The Adoption Handbook

Many people have contributed, knowingly or unknowingly, to my writing this book. I am deeply grateful to every one, but it would be too long a list to name you all personally.

I must, however, make an exception for a few people.

While putting on the finishing touches, my thoughts wander to Lucy, who so whole-heartedly worked to find the right words to reflect the spirit of this book. None of us knew by then that this would be her last translation. Regrettably, she lost her life in a tragic accident before she could complete her work. I am very grateful to Barbara for helping me out in such sad circumstances, by editing Lucy's work.

I realise that it cannot have been an easy task.

How can I ever thank Father d'Agostino, Protus, Nicolas, and the staff of Nyumbani for their never-ending support, their warmth and confidence. On a different note, I would like to thank Ester Meyer and Perry Pierik, from Aspekt, for the pleasant and open interaction, and their courage to publish my work in the English language.

For privacy reasons some people's names have been changed.

And last, but certainly not least, I thank my husband. Without his enthusiasm, his stimulating words and the room he gave me so that I may do this, there would be no book. Dearest, thank you.

Geeri Bakker

The Adoption Handbook

Handling stress during the adoption period

2006 Uitgeverij Aspekt

For Mette and Wisse

my back is strong enough
to carry you
in my dreams

but I must wait
until you are here
and I
can see you.

The Adoption Handbook
Original title: Het adoptieboek
© Geeri Bakker
Translation: Lucy Hayden
Editing: Barbara Plomp
2006 Uitgeverij ASPEKt
Amersfoortsestraat 27, 3769 AD Soesterberg, Nederland
info@uitgeverijaspekt.nl - http://www.uitgeverijaspekt.nl
Cover design: Aspekt Graphics
Setting and layout: Paul Timmerman, Amersfoort
Printing: Krips b.v. Meppel

ISBN 90-5911-315-2

All rights reserved. No part of this publication may be reproduced in any form or by any means without written permission of the publisher.

Contents

Foreword by Prof. Dr. R.A.C. Hoksbergen	7
Introduction	9
Part one; my story	15
Part two; step by step, handling stress	117
The procedure	119
What is stress?	126
Stress during the adoption procedure	130
Adoption versus pregnancy	135
Relationship under pressure?	140
Emotions	145
Disappointment = pain	152
Disappointment = sadness	157
Letting go of sadness and pain	163
Letting go to go forward	166
Mourning	172
Get yourself fit	176
Company	181
Choosing and being chosen	185
That far away country	191
Profile sketch of an adoptive parent	195
A child of your own	198
Make yourself at home	200
Final growth	203

Foreword by prof dr R. Hoksbergen

More and more adoptive children, now adults, and adoptive parents tell us about their experiences, about their lives as part of the adoption triangle. Their creative expressions are extremely useful for all involved with the placements of children for adoption, for the children themselves, and for their biological and adoptive parents. And let us not forget the professionals, sometimes called upon to improve the situation in the family or to support the adoptees.

The adoption process starts long before the child is placed into the family.

Geeri Bakker the author of this book "the adoption handbook" has had the courage to describe in detail from the beginning on, how she was able to adopt two African children. Indeed, she leads us through her complicated adoption process step by step.

After some years of trying to conceive without any success, the couple decides to try modern technology of procreation, and as many later adoptive parents, first In Vitro Fertilization. But after several attempts this also fails.

Then they come to the decision to adopt a foreign child. They have acquaintances in Kenya
 and with the help of these people they might be able to adopt a child. But then the adventure really starts, the fight against bureaucracy, against people not really interested in the benefits of a child.

Her feelings, uncertainties, all ups and downs during their adventures in Kenya are comprehensively disclosed. The Dutch side in the adoption process is rather positive. They get help from an agency involved, and from friends.

The second part of the book consists of research among a group of adoptive parents. Emotional aspects during the process of adoption is the main theme. Rationally and clearly she gives us information about the way parents deal with the emotions involved. Especially the aspect of *stress* of adoptive parents during the time before the actual placement of the child, the influence of the adoption adventure on the mutual relations of the parents, and emotions like fear, anger, grief, get a lot of attention.

The book is easy to read, and very practical. The first part is even an exciting read, about how, and when the couple will be able to come to a positive conclusion. Will they be able to adopt the child?

In short, this book is a useful and a meaningful addition to books on adoption, in particular for aspirant adoptive parents.

René Hoksbergen
(em. professor and adoption specialist)

Introduction

Can an adoption procedure be compared to anything?

This is a difficult question to answer, as each adoption procedure is different. Even when one family has adopted several children in separate procedures from the same country, you can still have the feeling of being thrown in at the deep end with each step. Some glide effortlessly through the adoption procedure as over a tranquil lake, whereas others feel they are being engulfed and forced under by the wild, uncontrollable waves. Then there are those for whom adopting is best compared with jumping in at the deep end. For us it resembled a long walk with a distinct lack of signs to show us the way. Just when we thought our destination was in sight we discovered the distance we still had to go. The sadness often felt like muscle cramps, and our spirits fell as we realised how distant our goal seemed, at times almost unattainable. We were often ignorant of the procedures that awaited us, but every new shoot of adrenaline helped us to persevere. Almost all adoption procedures have their surprises, whether pleasant or not. Each preparation for adoption tells a special story, long before the child arrives.

How do you deal with the constant alternation of anticipation, disappointment, suspense, waiting, and fighting to prove you are right – a Don Quixote feeling. The child has yet to arrive and you are sure it will all turn out fine, but it is so easy to lose heart along the long trek through the adoption procedure.

Various motives could set you off on your trek through the land of adoption. It might be the answer to a fertility problem, or perhaps you are fulfilling a long-cherished wish to give a disadvantaged child a chance of a better life. The ups and downs on the journey to the ultimate happiness of a pregnancy are well documented. There is plenty of reading material on nausea, tiredness, burping, pelvic instability, weight gain and other sources of discomfort. A child's growth is monitored by ultrasound scans and its heartbeat can be heard. Countless books have been written on the subject. A trap easy to fall into when trying to adopt is imagining yourself happy and safe on a long journey. Little has been said on the subject and thus little is known to prospective adoptive parents about the obstacles they may encounter on the journey to adoption. It may well be that you do not want to hear or see them. Perhaps you grit your teeth and keep walking and only at the end of the long road see the large blisters on your feet or feel the muscle pain that has been hampering your pace. Instead of a walk through a lovely forest on an evenly paved road where brightly coloured signposts guide your way, this more closely resembles a triple marathon. Endless walking to reach the reward awaiting you at the very end. At times you get so tired that you cannot appreciate the beauty of your surroundings, you feel sick with misery and have to rest. You take a break by the side of the road. Someone stops to lean over you, asks if you need help. Another tends to your blisters, a third to your stiffened muscles, and off you go again, on to your goal. It is the only thing on your mind, your reason for going through all of this. This road through the land of adoption will eventually lead you to your goal, your child. But one step at a time.

It is time that more attention is given to the stress that faces prospective parents during their long wait for their adoptive child, the child that is at the centre of the whole process. Although this is a good thing, one should not forget to name and acknowledge the not so happy feelings that adoptive parents-to-be have to endure. Little or nothing has been said to date of the disappointment, tension, sadness, anger, fear, impatience or powerlessness that so often characterise adoption procedures. Nothing in the literature addresses these issues directly. Hoksbergen, a well-known figure in writings about adoption, states in one of his books: "Ultimately, one consciously chooses to have a child who is not their own flesh and blood, and by the same token chooses to undergo drawn-out, expensive and often exasperating procedures." For him, that settles the matter. For many others, it is only the beginning.

As part of my dissertation 'Stress During the Adoption Procedure', which concluded my studies as a stress consultant, I asked a large number of adoptive parents about their experiences regarding stress during the adoption procedure. It turned out to be an unexplored territory.

Positive emotions were few and far between; pain from the past abounded, as did stress (negative tension). This motivated me to immerse myself in the subject and, at the request of many, write a book about it.

This is our story. We were able to adopt two children. We would have greatly appreciated being better prepared for coping with the repeated setbacks. We certainly did not always look after ourselves well. My aim is to help others who are about to embark on the same journey, or have already set off, so that they are better equipped to experience the adoption procedure in a more positive way. This book will help to put things into perspective. It offers support in difficult moments. It provides a different approach to dealing with the long wait. It is a plea to adoption advisors and those working in adoption to be more understanding. It invites relatives and friends to stand even more firmly by the parents-to-be. The time has come to expand the range of books written about natural pregnancies and now also prepare adoptive parents for the experience of *their* 'pregnancy' and 'childbirth'. This book will not make the adoption procedure any more enjoyable, but it may well help you to assume a different attitude throughout and look back on it later in a more positive light. This can help to prevent physical or mental problems when your child finally arrives and the tension subsides. Being better prepared means being able to more enjoy that initial period of time together, which will benefit both you and your child tremendously.

That is what this book is about. The question is not: "Do you have to prepare yourself for the adoption procedure?" but rather: "How can you prepare yourself for it?" It is certainly not my intention to put people off adoption by elaborating on all the problems that are likely to occur. How many people let themselves be put off from the "choice" of a natural pregnancy by disadvantages such as morning sickness, heartburn or backache, let alone the more serious problems which could occur during pregnancy, such as pelvic instability or toxaemia? The aim of this book is simply to help you to prepare as well as possible for this special period of your life. The wonderful child will come. You can put the flags out, send off the baby shower invitations, and get the champagne out. But first the adoption procedure.

The first part of this book consists, as explained earlier, of our own adoption story, which aims to serve as a reference to support the advice that follows. It has been written as an individual story to be read in one go. Later, passages in the second part will refer back to it to illustrate and elucidate.

The second part draws heavily on my experiences in our practice for natural healthcare. For several years now, my husband and I have been working in this practice with disciplines such as acupuncture, Bach flower remedies, foot reflexology, aroma massage, Reiki and stress therapy (with the specialised programme "stress during the adoption procedure").

Our experience in all these disciplines teaches us that balance in life, both physical and mental, is a magic key word. Such balance can prove particularly shaky and is often hard to establish and sustain during the years an adoption procedure may take.

The second part of the book aims to help you to identify exactly where the rub is. It aims to illustrate that your own individuality influences the way you experience the adoption procedure, your pregnancy. This certainly applies to women, of course, but to no lesser extent to men. You are both equally pregnant during the adoption procedure!

Just as each pregnant woman experiences pregnancy and childbirth in her own unique way, so does each prospective adoptive parent experience an adoption in his or her own way.

It is high time to expand on all the wise books about pregnancy and childbirth and take an in-depth look at the unique time around the adoption procedure, our pregnancy.

The second part of the book contains sections in italics. These will usually be comments from other adoptive parents, people with the same mission. You will also find some exercises to do either alone or together. The exercises aim to provide clarity, not to pass judgement or make you feel insecure.

At the end of this book, you may well literally be a few years further on and look back on the adoption procedure feeling glad and content. In that case, the book will have fulfilled its purpose. You will feel that you and your partner are up for your next journey: the journey through life with your child.

1
What came first

And a woman who held a babe against her bosom said
"Speak to us of Children."
And he said:
Your children are not your children.
They are the sons and daughters of Life's longing for itself.
They come through you but not from you,
And though they are with you, yet they belong not to you.

From: *The Prophet* by Kahlil Gibran.

When I look back on the turbulent years of the adoption procedures for our two children, it seems that they just flew by. The strange thing is that while we were in the middle of them, there seemed to be no end to an hour's wait before we could continue on our crusade. Waiting and struggling, seven years of our lives were marked by these two words more than any other. And they certainly exhausted us. It was only after the adoptions that the exhaustion manifested itself, through headaches and insomnia. Only then did we realise how much adrenaline had accumulated in every cell of our bodies.

Feelings of powerlessness, sadness, fear, anger, joy, impatience, irritation – the complete list would easily fill a page – had dominated our lives for years. Feelings that we were not fully aware of at the time and which only really sank in much later. We did not often stop to think about what was happening, because we were caught up in the whirlpool of the river that is adoption. We whirled along in it, and where there was an undercurrent we fought our way out of it. We gasped for air when we felt stifled, unaware of how the stress was sapping our strength.

Before the beginning of the adoption procedure, after everything we had been through with hospital visits, we did not think for one minute that the adoption procedure itself could possibly deal us so many blows. Had we realised, we might have prepared ourselves better physically and mentally, would have expressed our anger more freely (or even acknowledged the anger at all), would have taken more rest and enjoyed the breaks more consciously. We may have sought the warmth of fellow-sufferers more often. It may well have resulted in less severe after-effects – but we would certainly have persevered as we did.

The result of our perseverance are two wonderful children who are a joy to watch as they play, paint, cut, climb, quarrel or simply sleep. Two children who were worth every moment of waiting and struggling.

This book is meant for anyone who is directly or indirectly involved in adoption. First and foremost prospective adoptive parents and their friends and relatives, but also social workers involved, and the authorities directly influencing the unique period preceding the actual adoption. This book helps to make you more resilient as you enter this period and better able to deal more efficiently with whatever is thrown in your path. The ultimate aim is that you may look back on this unique period in your life with pleasure. This book is a pregnancy guide for adoptive parents-to-be.

Our own adoption story in the first part of this book will illustrate the second, which gives advice, insight and support, and suggests exercises for dealing with stress during the adoption procedure.

Adoption happens step by step.

1995 - 1998

We met while travelling on duty. We had both been working for KLM for many years, he was a purser and I a stewardess, and we met while enjoying a wonderful trip to San Francisco with a group of colleagues. My future husband soon had clear ideas about where he would like our meeting to lead. I, however, did not share his preoccupation at the time and once back home only renewed our acquaintance to take French lessons from him. He turned out to be a man well versed in many fields: teacher of French and German, purser with KLM, and with an interest in natural healthcare. One thing soon led to another and before long it was more than just French lessons which brightened our meetings. A few months later, I took my boyfriend home to meet the family.

My father put a lot of effort into pronouncing his name correctly. After a few months, he advised us to start thinking seriously about moving in together. Neither of us was particularly home-based, each with our own apartment and of course the weekly trips with KLM. Still, it was no easy task to bring together the very individual paths of two not-so-young lovers. I eventually gave up my flat and moved temporarily to Amsterdam. With the help of my private teacher, I obtained the rest of the language diplomas I needed for promotion, performed to the company's satisfaction in the psychological test, and after the final interview became assistant purser, Writser's right-hand woman. What a team!

The fact that I was not as fertile as I would have liked had already come up after our first kisses, but Writser did not consider that a problem. This situation was different. My first marriage had been childless but it would not happen again.

So off we set to the hospital and back it was to the medical grind. As a DES daughter, I had already established rather intimate contact with the department of gynaecology and fertility at the hospital during my previous marriage and I can hardly say I was looking forward to returning. After ten years mine was a well-known face. I had an intense wish to have a child, encouraged by fresh hope with this new man at my side. I was subjected to the ghastly examinations once again, but it appeared that there had been some positive anatomical changes, and an operation was considered a good start. But the minor abdominal operation unexpectedly became a major one, and when I came round from the anaesthetic, feeling quite miserable, I found a very worried Writser at my side. The gynaecologist announced some minutes later that the operation had been successful but had taken three and a half hours instead of twenty minutes. My stay in hospital was longer than planned, but we were strangely relieved that it had not been for nothing.

The next step was a series of injections. An artificial menopause was induced and I was introduced to the world of night sweats, day sweats, irritability, weight gain, headaches and all the other conditions. It was horrible. I hardly recognised myself. All for a good cause; all to make way for other hormones. Then came the Intra-Uterine-Insemination (or IUI, for the laypersons among you: artificial insemination) programme, which included artificial hormonal stimulation, ultrasounds, and the natural (meaning in this case through the finest of tubes) insertion of semen, timely ejected into a jar. When that failed to deliver the desired result, a little courage and a lot of despair sent us off on the joyless path of the circus that is in-vitro fertilisation, or IVF, i.e. fertilisation outside of the womb in a laboratory dish. In this way, we could at least rest assured that we had tried everything. The last thing we wanted was to reach the age of fifty and regret not having exhausted all the options.

As a DES daughter, I was naturally wary of all the extra hormones. In the fifties and sixties, the drug DES had frequently been given to women who wanted to have children and had miscarried in the past or ran the risk of miscarriage. The drug had been presented as a wonder drug by the pharmaceutical industry, but years later proved to be fatal for some of the daughters born from these pregnancies. These daughters, and later also the sons, were diagnosed with problems relating to fertility and other conditions (the use and effects of the drug diethylstilbestrol for the prevention of miscarriages are actually questioned). The DES foundation's court case against the pharmaceutical industry still continues in 2006 as compensation sums are being negotiated. Thus each form of hormonal stimulation was a subject of discussion between the gynaecologist and myself. So well did I understand the DES mothers who wanted to have a child desperately enough to eagerly take the wonder drug, oblivious to the consequences it would have for their children. But the IUI failed. I had never been pregnant, and I was not getting any younger, so we pressed ahead at the fertility outpatient clinic with IVF.

By this time we did feel at ease there, which is a good thing, for IVF is no picnic, and that is putting it mildly. We were lucky with our gynaecologists. Equipped with good humour, we went back and forth to the hospital where I opened my legs to undergo the umpteenth internal scan. We cried and we laughed. We knew why we cried, and we laughed simply because one cannot cry all day. Not that this was much help, because one simply does not want to be constantly preoccupied with the whole thing. A person cannot handle too much pain, so we stayed as level-headed as possible. So level-headed, in fact, that one day I went for a regular check-up ultrasound on my own. It was a three-minute routine procedure to count the number of egg-cells that had been produced by that stage. After a few ultrasounds you know what you are watching out for, and I immediately saw that where there should have been beautiful little dark eggs, there was nothing more than a large blackness.

The gynaecologist was sent for and he told me that things were not looking good, another cyst had grown instead of eggs and it would have to be removed instantly. Those were the moments that I wondered what on earth we were doing to ourselves. Perhaps it was even the moment that we decided to change course and started talking along different lines. I do not remember exactly. The IVF attempt had failed, the ten-centimetre cyst was suctioned off and I went home in tears. We did attempt a few more, but our hearts were no longer in it, even though each IVF attempt remained a cool oasis of warm hope.

Suddenly our conversations were about which was more important: a child of our own or that of another. Was this about our egos? Were we such unique people that the world would be a better place if there were more of our sort? What did we really want? How strong was our desire to take on the responsibility of bringing up a child – and one that was not our own flesh and blood? How much room did we want to create in our lives to give a child the space it needed to be itself? These were quite different conversations. Conversations about adoption.

I would like to mention at this point that years before (in 1991), I had started supporting an orphanage in the region of Nairobi, the capital of Kenya. Using the possibilities that the position of stewardess offers, a colleague and I had become actively involved. With the help of several other colleagues, this ultimately developed into a foundation, and since 1995, we have been involved in three orphanages in and around Nairobi. When Writser and I met, he soon fell under the spell of working with the Kenyans and a miracle happened: he too fell in love with these people with their amiable nature, their sense of humour and their irrepressible optimism. He also became a member of the board of 'our' foundation, the Kenya Orphan Foundation (SWK), making him almost a little Kenyan himself. (One of our 'own' orphanages occasionally offered children up for adoption.)
Our wish to have children proved to be strong. The desire to produce our

own children, which had for so long ruled our hearts and minds, had now ceased to be our primary concern. We were determined to focus on Kenya for adoption. After all, we felt attached to this country, we had a special relationship with its people, with whom we could share our tears and laughter. We felt at home with them. And yes, we were biased. We had met so many lovely people there, Kenyans and Mzungus (white people), who had taught us to look on the Kenyans with their possibilities and their impossibilities. We had learned so much from them.

Meanwhile, we were still involved with the last of the IVF hormonal hazards when we went for registration at the Dutch Ministry of Justice. A good start to the year 1998. My father blinked tears from his eyes when we told my parents about the step we had taken. It came as no surprise to my mother or many of our friends; after all, we had been involved with the orphans in Kenya for such a long time that the desire to adopt a child from that country was the logical next step on the journey we had embarked on long ago.

Once, some time before, my mother had been with us on a trip to this beautiful country. We had stayed in Nairobi for several days and she had had the opportunity to visit the orphanages with us. This had been a very special experience both for her and for us, because she knew Nyumbani, and so the adoption would hold that extra dimension for her, as well. From that trip onwards, my mother also felt a bit Kenyan and she dearly loved the dark little children who all called her "mama Geeri".

We continued the celebration of our marriage on 14 February 1998. Six weeks previously, we had taken the first step towards adoption, our new-year's resolution for 1998.

We had married in September of the year before, but were not spared the saddest of scenarios: Writser's father died after a very short but serious illness one week before our wedding day. After discussing the situation with Writser's mother, we decided to go ahead with the marriage, precisely because more than ever, we felt like husband and wife after that sad month of August. Being only boyfriend and girlfriend no longer reflected the depth of what we felt for each other. In our wedding invitations we called ourselves travelling companions, and that is what we still are, now enriched with two additional travellers. After the sober ceremony in September with our family and friends, we continued our nuptial journey on Valentine's Day. A day to celebrate our friendship, where we had the rings presented in Kenyan bowls. It almost felt as if a child of ours was already there with us.

But it was still early days. As the IVF attempts were coming to an end, our quest through the land of adoption began.

1998

As said, our New Year's resolution for 1998 was to register for adoption. Such an undertaking is actually fairly risk-free. You lose money if you go back on your decision, but at least you will have taken that first step. After a telephone call to the Ministry of Justice, we received a form by post requesting various sorts of information. No big deal – they want to know who you are, what you are, your relation to your partner (married status preferred), and what you want to be (parents). We returned it and were sent confirmation of receipt – rather quickly actually, in a matter of fourteen days – and a so-called BPK registration number. The date of receipt determines the number: the lower the number the better, which is no surprise in the bureaucratic Netherlands. A brochure on adoption procedures was the start to our waiting. The letter we received from the Ministry of Justice announced a waiting period of two years until the family interviews. This meant that Writser would be forty-one by the time we were finally presented to the Child Protection Agency. It would also mean that we would no longer be eligible to adopt a baby. Dutch legislation stipulates that there must be no more than forty years between the age of the eldest adoptive parent, in our case Writser, and the child to be adopted, at the moment of its arrival in the Netherlands. But a child of one or two would also be fine for us. Yet every month counted, for studies show that younger children have a much better chance of bonding.

The wording of letter was rather unsympathetic. Taking into consideration the fact that over 90% of applicants are childless against their will, a sentence such as: "It must also be noted that no couple can be given the absolute guarantee that after obtaining "consent in principle" a child will actually be placed", is rather harsh (as the authors of the letter agree, considering the following sentence), not to mention discouraging. Is it really necessary or desirable to take this tone? A sentence such as: "Taking in a foreign foster child without a valid consent in principle is a criminal offence", seems uncalled-for, particularly as it appears in the very first letter that aspiring parents receive. One can only guess at the reasons the authors have for making this point.

The next step that has to be taken is a financial one. At the time, we had to pay close to 400 euros for the application.

So let's see what this buys you.

Six compulsory information afternoons organised by the Ministry of Justice. Attending these meetings is so important that your employer is obliged to grant you leave.

We were lucky enough to find ourselves in a wonderful group. We shared the same wry sense of humour that we had developed from years on the medical treadmill, knowing better than anyone how much cc is needed in a syringe on the ninth day of an IVF attempt – a good question for trivial pursuit. It was also the first time that we had ever sat together with fellow-sufferers. What we had in common as a group was the determination to maintain a positive and constructive approach to the meetings.

To avoid the traffic congestion between Rotterdam and our home, we travelled to Rotterdam by train on those six afternoons, something we would not normally do. On the way there normal conversation was still possible, but on the way home it was all weary talk of what we had been made afraid of on that particular day. As far as I can remember, the emphasis was on the type of problems that adoptive children could encounter upon arrival with the Dutch family. The letter from the Ministry of Justice runs also along these lines: "One of the aims of the general information provided by the Centre for Information on the Adoption for Foreign Children (VIA) is to inform the prospective adoptive parents about possible risks associated with adopting a foreign child (so that aspiring adoptive parents can make a well-considered decision about their family)". It would have been pleasant to be able to go home with a different feeling – not one of fear, but of happiness about the new possibilities. Instead of becoming afraid, though, we only became more resolute. We took the bull by the horns and remained steadfast on our chosen path. We found the most useful afternoon to be the one that dealt with the child's bonding upon arrival with the family. This was a theme to which we later always devoted special attention. We were shown films about orphanages in for example India, but because of our travels, they showed us nothing new. We particularly enjoyed the opportunity we had to show a film of the orphanage from which our child was to come. Unlike many other adoptive parents, we knew before the information afternoons began that Kenya was the country it would have to be, which made many of the themes superfluous for us, such as passing round photos and asking the group members where they thought a particular child came from. What struck us was that it often seemed to be the accessibility to a child that made parents choose a specific country. At the time, China was a country from which adoptions could be organised fairly quickly, and apart from our children and another child from Korea, all from our group adopted Chinese girls. After the VIA course you do not want to wait another four years to hold the child of your dreams in your arms. Age also plays a role for many people. A few of our group were rapidly approaching the age limit. Anyone who wanted to adopt two children was well advised to act quickly. Content aside, we found the afternoons useful for the process of growth towards parenthood. But above all, it was the friendly atmosphere, enhanced by Dutch delicacies such as liquorice and the meal we shared after the final meeting, which helped us to keep our spirits up. We still see some of the VIA course members at other arrival parties and reunions.

On 1 March, the meetings came to an end and we received a letter from the Ministry of Justice saying that our data had been sent to the Child Protection Agency in The Hague.

1999

We subsequently received a letter from the Child Protection Agency requesting a medical certificate and a certificate of good conduct from the Dutch Judicial Documentation Register. In other words: were we healthy, non-criminal parents-to-be?

19 April marked a big day. The first meeting took place in The Hague, so I did not have to tidy the house or replace the withered plants in the front garden. After all, if you cannot look after your house and garden, how are you supposed to look after a child?

All in all, the talks with the woman from the Child Protection Agency were not so bad. However, the reason seemed wrong in principle. It is nobody's business if we have rows from time to time, or how we solve them. It is nobody's business at all what our relatives think about our having a child. And it is nobody's business how we plan to bring up our child, whether we have thought about what school it will go to, or whether my husband and I share the same opinion on this or that subject in life. Other prospective parents are not asked these questions before they get pregnant, either, so why were we?

Incidentally, to correct a common misconception: no questions are asked about income. For a simple reason.

The adoption procedure has not been designed to accommodate the financial capacities of couples on state benefits or minimum wage, unless they win the lottery. So there was no need for that question.

I know of people who, without even having a strong emotional wish, found themselves having to save up for several years in order to be able to adopt a second child. This state of affairs horrifies me. It costs less to drive a brand new middle-class car than to pay for adoption fees, and who is in a position to buy a brand new car every eighteen months, anyway? If that is not selection, then I do not know what is.

After the VIA meetings, several things were happening at once.

First, the talks with the Child Protection Agency continued.
Second, we were involved in talks with the Association of Independent Adoptive Parents, because Kenya as a country is outside the possibilities that adoption agencies offer. We thus became what in Dutch are called "Do-It-Yourself", i.e. independent adoptive parents.
Third, we had talks with adoption agencies in search of the agency that would ultimately verify our contact address abroad, that is, the address from which we wanted to adopt a child. We ended up with the Dutch-based Africa Foundation.

On 18 January, we sent a letter to the Africa Foundation requesting that they verify our contact address, the orphanage Nyumbani. The 1993 Dutch Placement of Foreign Foster Children Act describes the task of a licensed adoption agency for independent adoptive parents such as ourselves. The Act is quite wordy, but comes down to the DIY adopters having to submit the adoption documents relevant for the procedure to the licence holder. The subsequent investigations are aimed at the reliability and thoroughness of the foreign authorities, institutions or persons designated by the aspiring adoptive parents. Pages and pages of details follow. Of course, the verification of such an address is of utmost importance and so we do fully support this procedure. However, it was the first time that the Africa Foundation had found itself confronted with the task of socalled partial mediation as an agency, which made the process arduous and slow. I will come back to the subject later.

Fourth, in mid-April we received an e-mail from Nyumbani saying that a girl had been brought in who would probably be available for adoption at some point in the future. As a result of years of regular visits for the Kenyan Orphans Foundation, we had become close acquaintances of the founder, the manager and the social worker, who were all aware of our wish to adopt from their orphanage.

Nyumbani is a special orphanage, as it cares for HIV positive babies and children. A number of small babies placed in the orphanage may be pronounced healthy during the first year of their lives, or shortly after, for a child's auto-immune system can triumph over the virus. From then on, this child's risks of becoming infected with HIV are the same as a healthy child's. In most cases, these children have been abandoned by their mothers who were either too sick or otherwise unable to care for their children. Relatives of these women often cannot be found. They will not look after mother or child for fear of AIDS and they do not respond when a search for the abandoned children's mothers, fathers or relatives is carried out. AIDS is a major problem in Kenya, due mainly to the substantial gulf between Kenyan culture and the use of contraceptives necessary to prevent AIDS. An unrealistic fear of infection via normal human contact often keeps relatives at a distance. As a result, no one wants to take in a child who has been declared healthy and so another children's home awaits it.

As there had been adoptions to European parents before, everyone in Nyumbani was confident that an adoption to the Netherlands was possible. The Nyumbani people were even collecting data for us from a previous adoption by an Italian couple.

22 April 1999

22 April was the date of my first meeting with Salomé, the girl they had told me about in the e-mail. I happened to have a journey to Kenya on my schedule and despite the fact that Writser could not accompany me, we decided that I would go to Nyumbani alone. In retrospect, this was a strange situation, but in the heat of the moment our insatiable curiosity prevented us from realising that we would not be sharing this unique moment. It was all very unreal. All of a sudden there was this e-mail saying there was a girl who could perhaps become our daughter, and a rather casual invitation to "come and have a look". Then came the perfect flight schedule. Looking back, I went to Nyumbani in a rather naïve state of mind. A colleague went with me, as colleagues had often accompanied us in the past when going to look at projects. Although it may seem strange to an outsider, it was wonderful to have her with me. Not just anyone, but someone who had come to share something special with me. And so off I set, photo and video cameras in hand. Unaware of the full implications of what I was about to experience, and in a state of childlike excitement and curiosity, we arrived at Nyumbani.

Unlike previous, very informal occasions on which I was free to walk around wherever I wanted, I was now ushered into a room to talk to Nicolas, the social worker. Looking back on those days, from the moment I received the e-mail to the journey and those first moments in Nyumbani, my memories seem enveloped in mist, and tears still well up in my eyes when I think of myself in that small room. Although she was already five months old, she was but a tiny bundle, weighing not even ten pounds, when she was brought in. We did not know at the time that she had weighed less than three and a half pounds at birth. Nicolas laid her in my arms. Lots of blanket, a beautiful little head and the biggest eyes I had ever seen. Eyes that were looking at me. She had never seen me before, but her eyes locked on mine never to let go. My eyes filled with tears, and they flowed over her like an unstoppable stream of liquid love. From that moment Salomé was my child. The only thing missing in this perfect moment was Writser, but how could we have known a few weeks ago, when the flight schedules were arranged, that this journey was to be so special… In thought I knew he was there with me, I could feel him. That was the day she was born to us, 22 April 1999.

Not until much later did we find out that Nicolas's professional eye had been observing the 'match'. Had he not approved of what he saw, we would not have been able to adopt Salomé. But my infatuation, my love, was, and still is, perfectly sincere. I was holding a very special person in my arms. Her large dark eyes, deep black skin, tiny hands and feet, her beautiful mouth and cheeky little nose. She looked like a perfect doll, Snow White in black, and now our beautiful child.

I can hardly describe the mixed feelings I had as I returned to the crew hotel a few hours later. I was so glad that I had not been alone. One of my many colleagues had shared this special moment with me. She had taken photos of those first minutes. Photos later to be shown to the new father, the proud grandfather and grandmothers, and all of our relatives and friends. From that day onwards Salomé was part of the family, she belonged with us. I phoned Writser from the hotel. I cannot remember if I cried or not, I probably did. And once I was back in the Netherlands, the one-hour photo development service seemed to take forever.

When I was back home, we phoned flight schedule planning to ask for a flight to Kenya together in the following week. I had already been scheduled on a flight to Kenya and would it not be wonderful if the mom and dad-to-be could set off together. A good deal of rescheduling was required, but the goodwill and creativity of KLM were behind us and soon we set off together for the first meeting between father and daughter.

May 1999

We had manoeuvred ourselves into a strange position. At the second meeting with the Child Protection Agency, we already knew about our little girl and even had 'evidence' in the form of lovely photos. What was the best way to proceed? Keep quiet or be open? We opted for the latter, hoping that this might accelerate the procedure and the awarding of consent in principle. After all, now that we had seen Salomé, we had a clearer vision of our goal. Luckily, it all worked out. For the second meeting, our house was dust-free, the front garden thriving, and a photo of little Mette Joanne Salomé at the ready. After that, it was back to the office once more for the reading of the final report, and consent in principle was as good as ours. Oddly enough, one does not get to keep a copy of that wonderful report, allegedly to prevent improper use, whatever that may mean. Thus a probing, personal report is written about two adults (a work of art we would have liked to frame and hang over the nuptial bed, especially since it confirmed our qualities as parents), but it is not to go into the personal adoption scrapbook – instead, it is sent to the licence holder and that is where it stays. But on 7 June 1999, the consent in principle dropped on to the doormat. Another reason to go out for a celebratory meal.

The Africa Foundation did not give us much of a reason for celebration. As it was the first time that they were dealing with DIY adopters, they even needed to obtain the partial mediation form from the World Children Foundation. What's more, they did not know exactly was expected of them as partial mediator and all the way up until September insisted on the necessity of a Kenyan law governing foreign adoptions before they were prepared to even look at information about our chosen orphanage. But such a law, although it had been under negotiation for years, did not exist yet. There was, however, a law for adoptions within Kenya and we did actually manage to dig up this law, but that proved to be a complete waste of effort. It had to be a law governing foreign adoptions. That was what they wanted. But as there was no such thing, we struggled on until September 1999.

Letters, visits and telephone calls to the Dutch embassy in Kenya and other authorities failed to produce anything other than the legislation on Kenyan adoptions we had already found. After consulting the Association of Independent Adoptive Parents, we decided to hire a lawyer who specialised in adoption problems. Time was pressing, we were getting older, and our goal was being clouded by the haze of legislation. Fortunately, we had legal insurance, which now served us well. The insurance company even told us we could engage an adoption specialist, and a couple of letters to the Foundation and the Ministry of Justice were enough to get the approval procedure back on track. But we were extremely worried that it would not work out. After all, if the Netherlands were to refuse approval, our child would not be allowed to enter the country.

On 1 September, we sent every bit of information we could find about Nyumbani, including the link to its website, to the Africa Foundation and, while the court case for our child's adoption was already under way in a Kenyan court, we received the long-awaited letter from the Ministry of Justice that approved contact on 12 October. After all, the Africa Foundation was to send its approval to the Ministry of Justice, whereupon the Ministry would consent while closely monitoring all developments. Surprisingly enough, the procedure, prolonged by ignorance on the part of the authorities involved, was not detrimental to our relationship with them and we were able to have many positive conversations with the people at both the Ministry of Justice and the Africa Foundation. There was no ill-will at play, but the rules of the DIY adopters' game are not straightforward, which hinders the speed of the adoption process. At the expense of the child.

We were astounded by the fee of 680 euros administrative and partial mediation costs, particularly as we had provided and organised all documentation ourselves. Still, we never expected adoption to be cheap.

It feels like it was already October when these bureaucracy-bred events took place, but our fighting spirit was strengthened by the thought of our daughter Salomé.

May - September 1999

The second of May was the big day. We had arrived on duty in Nairobi the previous evening and on Sunday morning we left the hotel for Nyumbani at a quarter past nine. I felt quite tense, mostly because I knew what to expect, but I was anxious to see Writser's reaction to her.

When we arrived, I hurried like a proud mother to the house where Salomé lived.

Nyumbani was built on an existing compound and the surrounding land pertains to it. The centre originally consisted only of a single, large main building in which all the children lived together. A sectioned-off part of the large central room was reserved for the very sick children and I remember a request for an electric heater to keep the small children warm several years before. The large building is still standing although donations made it possible to realise the dream of Nyumbani's founder, Father d'Agostino: expanding the centre with several smaller, individual houses, each with its own 'mama', who fulfils a combination role of nurse and nanny. These houses could accommodate ten to twelve children who would be able to enjoy several happy years in a homely environment. This was the situation of some eighty children in Nyumbani, at the time that we were in the process of adopting Salomé.

Salomé lived in house 'Claire', but she was not to be found on that sunny Sunday morning. Her cot was empty and I did not understand why. It immediately occurred to us that she might be sick, but before we could dwell on this thought, we were welcomed by Protus, the centre's manager. We could not have picked a more special day to arrive, for unbeknown to us Salomé was to be baptised that very day!

Within five minutes we were sitting in the front rows of the church. Although it was not a real church building, it was the largest building on the site and as well as serving as a church, it was also used as a recreation room and classroom. Within the same five minutes we were hurriedly declared godparents, and Salomé was placed in our arms as Father d'Agnostino asked us with what names we would like to have her baptised.

We were completely dumbfounded. During our endless attempts at natural conception we had regularly talked about names, so we were luckily able to respond to Father d'Agostino's question with a harmonious answer: Mette Joanne Salomé Boelens.

Mette was chosen after my grandmother who was called Metje. Metje comes from Margaretha and means pearl. Although Mette actually means 'gathering place'. Later, as Mette grows older, we notice that she does indeed like to gather, especially people. Joanne was chosen after the first names of both of our parents (named Anne, Annet and Johannes (twice), respectively), and Salomé after her biological mother. All her roots are now included in her name. Both of us had always supported the idea of naming a child after a relative. We think it is a wonderful notion. This way we were able to honour those close to our hearts.

At the moment of adopting Mette, we were certain that given our age this was to be our only child. Not until later did we hear that we could adopt a second child.

So Mette now had a new name, and she indeed became a pearl in our existence, a reason for living. Deeply moved and astonished, I submerged myself in the baptism ceremony. My family were members of the Dutch reformed church, but I had always been moved by the wonderful, elaborate Sacrament of the Roman-Catholic ceremony of baptism. The anointment, the speaking of the name, the cross on the forehead, the baptism itself with lots of water, the baptism candles – which, incidentally, we had to return afterwards because of expenses. The video camera had broken the day before our departure, but Writser took lots of photos.

I think I had tears in my eyes throughout the entire mass. How I had always longed to be able to hold my own child up to be baptised. And now the moment had come, completely unexpectedly, in a building surrounded by children who would almost all die at too young an age. A small drum beat out a delightful rhythm to a song sung by the Nyumbani children. I will never forget that day. It was also special that Father d'Agostino was the one to perform the baptism. This short man with his huge charisma had helped us so much on our quest for all sorts of information. His presence on this extraordinary day gave us a deep feeling of comfort, of coming home.

After the ceremony, we had our photo taken and coincidentally, we had brought marshmallows to treat all the children. A party! We had a proper baptism party!

Mette was given her very first toy, a cuddly toy that she carried with her faithfully from that moment onwards. She also got a musical jumping jack from us which we attached to the side of her cot. It hangs on her bed at home to this day. A rattle, a soft book and her first toys were eagerly accepted. I also took the first photos of father and daughter, a small bundle in the arms of such a big man. Writser looked a little awkward, but that was sure to change with time. That evening we flew back to the Netherlands on duty with a new story to tell. A story too fantastic for words. Two weeks previously we had still been empty-handed, yet now we had our hands full. We were entangled in feelings, but above all they were feelings of joy and affection. We had made it: we had a child.

But things were not all hunky-dory. Deep down was a feeling of unease regarding Mette's health. Mette was born of a mother who was infected with HIV. That was all we knew. We did not know how serious the mother's condition was or how she had contracted HIV. The hospital where Mette was admitted found her to be carrying HIV antibodies. That was why she had been placed in Nyumbani; it was, after all, unclear whether she had actually been infected by her mother. In such a case, a child develops its own defence system during its first year. In Mette's case we had to wait patiently to see whether or not she would lose the antibodies from her mother within the first year of her life. It was a far-reaching decision to grow attached to a child that may turn out to be HIV positive, one consequence of which would be that we would not be able to adopt her. The Netherlands does not accept adoptive children who are suffering from a fatal illness. And yet from Nyumbani's first e-mail onwards, we decided to meet and become attached to Mette and to follow her on her voyage of discovery through life, regardless of what the future may bring. Often we were full of hope, at times we were anxious. Nyumbani understood this only too well and helped with positive stimuli. For example, in the e-mail that we received the day after the baptism, when we were back in the Netherlands, we were asked to spell the names again in full, Father d'Agostino's the last sentence was: 'She looks more and more negative to me.' This gave us hope for the future.

On 10 June, seven months after her birth, we received the good news we had been waiting for totally unexpectedly. We had been told that the final tests would not be performed until she was a year old, so we were amazed at the arrival of an e-mail. Five days later Writser went to visit Mette.

Meanwhile, the search for the adoption law was in full swing. We received a great deal of help from the embassy staff in Nairobi, for we had many acquaintances there who sympathised greatly with us and wanted to contribute in some way. However, as said, at the end of the day we needed to call in a Dutch lawyer to cast some light on this diffuse problem.

Then some more good news arrived. While we were caught up in the problems of getting contact approved in the Netherlands, the court case as part of the adoption procedure in Kenya entered its first phase of preparation following the issuing of Mette's certificate of good health. We met our lawyer, a wonderful Kenyan woman called Esther. She was experienced in adoption cases and gave us a list of necessary documents. There were twenty-one of them, varying from photocopies of passports, employer's declaration, medical certificates of the three of us, certificates of good conduct, birth certificates, statements of relatives attesting that they would take care of the child in case of our demise, etc. Legislation on Kenyan adoption states that the prospective adoptive parents must have looked after the child for three months. After negotiations with the lawyer and finally also the judge, the sum of our visits to Mette were considered to equal this length of time.

So we set about collecting the documents. It was quite a pleasant task as it gave us the feeling of doing something constructive. Although it remained overshadowed by the uncertainty of whether Mette would ever be able to enter the Netherlands, as the court case was still running, we felt great moral support from the Dutch lawyer who said that it should work out.

Summer brought even more surprises. A colleague approached us with the question of whether it was possible to adopt a child from Nyumbani. She had visited the place on her travels and she and her husband had also decided to adopt a child from the orphanage. That was a pleasant distraction and our problems could suddenly be discussed with another couple in the same situation. Their story also had a happy ending and in December 2002, Father d'Agostino was able to embrace three of his 'own' Nyumbani children when he was passing through the Netherlands for a few days.

By the end of September, we had collected all the papers. In Nyumbani, people had done their utmost to obtain police declarations, hospital certificates etc. with regard to Mette's background, and our papers were all ready, too. Thanks to frequent e-mailing, communication was fast and efficient, all the more so as we were in Kenya almost on a weekly basis to visit Mette.

October 1999

Things were getting more and more exciting. On the one hand, we were regularly visiting Mette and were able to hold her, play and eat with her, dress her and go for walks with her. On the other hand, there were the early morning visits to Esther. The advantage of the location of our hotel was its proximity to our lawyer. It took us five minutes to reach her office and Esther was usually on time.

Papers had to be signed for the court and we had to be present on certain dates. It must be said that our employer cooperated whenever necessary and reasonably possible, so that we could be present at all important moments. Of course, we had to organise most of it ourselves, but it made us feel good.

The first hearing was scheduled for 18 October. We needed a temporary guardian (*Guardian Ad-Litem*) and had asked Nicolas, the social worker, to take this upon himself. He was a wonderful, sympathetic person and an enormous source of support to us in trying times. There are few Kenyan men on whose shoulders I have cried, but Nicolas has certainly seen most of those tears. On each visit to Kenya we relived the same emotional strain, holding Mette in our arms or watching her as she lay in her cot before we had to leave her again. For a long time she seemed so close and yet so out of reach. Fortunately, Nicolas was glad to oblige and so on 18 October he was appointed by Esther as temporary guardian of our dear little Mette.

We later obtained all the court papers from Esther. It was strange to read how others had been observing us without our even noticing it. What had impressed the people in Nyumbani above all was the fact that we had begun the adoption procedure while it was still unclear if Mette was going to be healthy or not. Needless to say this was a precarious situation, but it had never been our biggest stress factor. (After all, in June had we already received the good news about Mette's health.) During the hearings, every one of our personal details was brought up. Our identities, nationalities, religion, health, work, financial situation, relatives, relationship, motives for adopting, beliefs on how to deal with racial issues, time to care for the child, nursing qualities (I had been a nurse for eleven years before going to work for KLM and this was certainly now useful on our parental CV), the bond we had established with Mette since May, and so on. We had not collected that mound of papers for nothing.

This particular hearing went swimmingly, which brightened our outlook for the final hearing on 26 October when the adoption was to be finalised.

I have not mentioned the adoption's expenses yet. Of course there was the initial 400 euros for the meetings and then the 860 more for the agency's partial mediation, but apart from that, expenses had been rather reasonable. Our occupation was a great help as it so often took us to the right place without travel cost. The lawyer eventually gave us a quite acceptable bill in which she claimed her hours, the cost of 'engaging' the court as well as the judge, and legal fees. We much appreciated being able to clearly see where our money had gone. No obscure charges, only clarity and transparency. Things were very different for Nyumbani. These people were our friends and did not want any money. They were so happy that one of their healthy children was going to a good home, that we were greeted with a warming handshake (Writser) and hearty hugs (Geeri) on every new visit. It is true that we did bring them presents now and again, such as a bottle of eau de toilette for Father d'Agostino and a watch for Protus. It was also very special for me to see how gratefully Nicolas accepted the smart clothes, once owned by my ever so thin father, which proved to be a perfect fit. He wore my father's waistcoat on special occasions just for me. And of course we brought sweets for the children, and clothes, games, rusks and baby food for Mette. With her sweet tooth (which she still has today), she loved those traditional Dutch current buns.

25 October 1999

On 25 October, we were getting ready to leave. Work took us to Nairobi, and we were to appear at Esther's office at eight o'clock the next morning . We later said to each other: "How did we manage to keep working through such emotional times?" I think it was to do with the special bond we had established with each other over the years. In the relatively short time since we had first met, Writser and I had gone through so much together that it sometimes felt unreal. The warmth and devotion we felt and the openness with which we talked about our feelings were the result of that. We had learned to cry together; in fact, we had made it into an art form. We had also had the support of many sympathetic colleagues with whom we could let off steam and then find the strength to return to our mission. I sometimes think that the motivation of always being able to return to Mette greatly boosted the quality of our work. We were driven by enthusiasm to make all the journeys to Kenya, which must surely have had a positive effect on the people around us. Occasionally, we had to muster our energy, but generally we were bursting with it. How many adoptive parents have the chance to slowly but surely grow towards that moment of actual adoption? Of course there is a shadow side to being so close to a goal you cannot quite reach. But it kept coming closer.

One journey was particularly special. We had sneaked into our suitcases a traditional Dutch delicacy eaten to celebrate a birth: round biscuits with candied aniseed sprinkles. As after tomorrow, the birth may just become a reality and after that, it would only be a matter of time until we could take Mette home with us. The crew gave us a mascot in the form of a small plush dog which proved a trusted companion to Mette for many years to come.

At eight o'clock, we were in Esther's office, both of us a bundle of nerves. "This judge could give us a hard time", Esther told us. He was a difficult man and notorious for splitting hairs. That did not exactly cheer us up. We were also given a strict code of conduct. Only Esther would talk to the judge; we should keep quiet. We were only to speak to him when explicitly addressed. Mette was brought in by Nicolas who after today would be absolved from guardianship if all went well. Mette had been dressed beautifully by mama Margareth, the woman who was her regular mama in Nyumbani. She was a lovely lady with a strong maternal instinct and a great sense of humour, who did a splendid job of looking after Mette. Mette was very attached to her. This was not so easy to deal with at this particular time and certainly not very practical on a day like today, as Mette had recently been taking a little more time to feel at ease with one of us. But we still remembered well what we had learned at the VIA meetings and were now sure that Mette was able to bond. Luckily, she was in a very affectionate mood on this particular day, and in convoy we set off on foot to the impressive court building, which was right around the corner.

Up until then I had never seen a court on the inside and had always enjoyed watching court scenes in English and American television series and films; a famous actor leaning coolly over the witness stand or talking to the jury in a low voice. The image was engrained in my mind, so it was a great disappointment to find just the one room for children and youth affairs. Before being allowed into the room, we were made to await our turn in a large room for hours, together with many Kenyans, also waiting.

I experienced a first advantage as a mother when I was offered to go and sit on one of the scarce benches with Mette sleeping in my arms. The scene has been immortalized in a beautiful photo of Mette holding her new toy dog and her green blanket, her comfort blanket, tightly.

Our turn came eventually, at about eleven o'clock. When the door opened, first of all came that disappointment of the sight of just one room with an enormous desk and an enormous judge. He took up the entire width of the desk from left to right and looked colossal. We were seated on another bench. For the occasion I was wearing my Esprit suit and Writser his bowtie (Esther's dress code). Mette had woken up and was watching the events with her large eyes.

Esther and judge Mogai were sitting opposite each other with that battleship-like desk between them. We were sitting a few metres away but they spoke so softly that we could not understand anything of what was said between them. Of course, Mette decided that the performance had gone on for long enough and started to whine. To avoid disturbing the important 'talks', we wondered what would be the best thing to do. We did not want to run the risk of putting ourselves at a disadvantage. Should I go for a walk and risk being punished for it, or should I stay put and risk Mette's volume being heard two corridors down? I opted for the former and hesitantly got up and took Mette to look at the pictures on the wall.

The strange thing was that the judge, that harsh-looking man, was charmed by this move and pronounced the adoption finalised, as Esther told us later. What was also strange, was that although I was generally so alert to what was going on, I was oblivious to the fact that, as we stood outside after the hearing, the adoption was in the bag. I had been so involved with trying to distract Mette that I had completely missed the judge's pronouncement.

At last Mette was our daughter!

The birth was now a fact, although, as we later learned, we would still have to wait before we were able to take her home with us. But on that 26th of October, we did not give that a second's thought.

There was champagne in Esther's office, a phone call home and of course a fresh pile of forms to fill in. Then off to Nyumbani to share the good news, and our glorious day was complete. The journey home to the Netherlands was one big celebration as well, and the traditional biscuits with aniseed sprinkles had never tasted so good.

When we got back to our house the flag was flying, the room was full of flowers and cards; at long last there was a reason to celebrate.

Everyone shared in our happiness.

November 1999

From the day of the judge's decision our lives never stopped moving forward. We had now received approval from the Netherlands. With the help of all the information we could give them, the Africa Foundation had checked our contact address and declared it reliable. They had also contacted Nyumbani of their own accord and obviously had found no grounds for any objections to granting their approval. And since we also had approval from the Kenyan court, what else could possibly stand in our way? We started preparing the baby's room. We had chosen some items a few months previously and with regard to delivery had an agreement that should the adoption fall through or the Netherlands refuse to issue the immigration warrant, we would not have to buy the goods. But we no longer saw any problems and went and bought what we had ordered and were given many things by friends. A cot with a matching chest of drawers and bookshelf, a car seat, high chair, play pen, plate, cup, spoon, fork, nappies, pram and buggy. The complete baby kit. We picked the wallpaper and the cards to announce the new arrival and at the same time kept travelling back and forth to Kenya. 14 November would be Mette's first birthday, but our plans to celebrate this day in the Netherlands had to be revised.

On 10 November, we sent an e-mail to Protus asking him to get in touch with Esther as she was not answering our urgent questions. There was a problem with a delay in Mette's immigration papers, which had to be approved for Nairobi by the Dutch visa department. The embassy in Nairobi announced that certain papers were missing, like Mette's birth certificate. This was well possible, for Mette had been left at the hospital by her mother without any documentation of birth. Therefore, an alternative had to be found. Enter Nicolas.

On 19 November, we received the news that the Kenyan authorities were in possession of all the necessary and duly certified documents.

Mr. Odhiambo from the passport department would ensure that the processing went smoothly. Shortly after, we received another e-mail asking whether we could come to stay for a longer period of time to sort some more things out. We were starting to get quite nervous being so far away in the Netherlands. It looked as though everything was going according to plan, but the final touches were costing us more energy that we had foreseen.

In the Netherlands, we had extensive contact with the visa department via fax and e-mail to organise all Dutch documents before setting off to Nairobi on what could well be a longer visit. There were never enough hours in a day.

On 16 November, it was party time in Nyumbani. Mette's first birthday was celebrated. Admittedly, it was a couple of days after the actual day, but at one year of age she will not have realised. Together with Protus and Nicolas we had organized a big party, both to celebrate Mette's birthday with some of the other children and as an early farewell party.

There were cakes, Dutch sweets, crisps, lemonade, and more. We had been given party hats and little flags by a fast-food chain in the Netherlands, and everything looked festive. Mette had her very first cake and got it all over herself. We looked on as doting parents, albeit with a certain sense of apprehension, for at that point nothing was really prepared for the actual farewell, the departure from Kenya and the arrival in the Netherlands.

Back in the Netherlands, Writser went to buy the tickets for Mette's journey home. As KLM staff we fly at reduced rates if seats are available. These stand-by tickets still needed to be paid for. That in itself was no problem, but we had to buy a ticket for Mette as well. As a baby, she would not be travelling on a full ticket, but a baby seat would have to be paid for. But it was not even as easy as that, because the final decision of a Kenyan judge is not sufficient proof of adoption for the Netherlands. After all, she was not yet registered as our child with any authority. However fortunately, thanks to KLM's unwavering support, the matter was sorted out and we eventually were in possession of travel papers for the three of us.

On 22 November, we were unexpectedly asked to contact the visa department again. It transpired that the names that had been passed on to the Dutch embassy were the names Mette had had before the baptism, namely Salomé Wanja, and not her new names which were pronounced when the judge finalised the adoption. We were due to depart on 23 November, so we had to solve the problem that day. It is far more difficult trying to get official matters organised in Nairobi than in the Netherlands. To our great relief the visa department was willing to help us with this problem at short notice, although we did not know the final outcome before we set off on the twenty-third of November. The definitive approval of Mette's adoptive names was finally waiting for us at the embassy in Kenya upon our arrival.

We set off, buggy and all. And thank goodness, there was room on the plane. Thoroughly spoilt by our colleagues, we arrived in Kenya.

During the flight I wrote the following poem:

beautiful girl
with your eyes so wide
we're on our way
to take you in
so you can travel
travel with us

with you
we continue our journey
with you
we start a new life

our life with a baby's room
a play pen and an intercom
dolls and nappies

our life is transformed
so wanted
so welcome
so wonderful
you don't know
what awaits you
you don't know
what changes will come
will you be cold
or quiet…
will you miss them
your friends…
Margareth, sister Matron,
Nicolas and Protus
will you feel alone…

you don't know
not yet
and we hope
that your youth
will dissolve
the pain of parting

we hope
that you will be happy
and cheerful and free
to be who you want
to become
what you want

we hope
that you will love us

*that we can be
a good mom and dad
to you
we hope
that we can implant
into your heart
into your being
the love we already feel*

*we're on our way
to fetch you
what a miracle
what a gift from God
thank you God*

our happiness is complete.

The next day, we went with Esther to see Mr. Odhiambo. There was a lot of ado before we managed to get to see him, and we ended up staying there nearly all day. Yet all for nothing: we did not get the papers we thought we needed. At least that is what Esther and Nicolas said. Later that day, we also went to the Dutch embassy. They had very nearly finished preparing the papers, which would most probably be completed by the next morning. They also told us that Mette would not need anything else and that we should not worry about Mr. Odhiambo's papers. But in Nyumbani they told us an entirely different story. We would be stopped at customs on suspicion of kidnapping; we risked being put in jail, Mette would have to go back to Nyumbani and would of course never be able to go to the Netherlands after that. And the orphanage would be questioned on the matter and be stripped of its reputation. Such confusion could exist because no one, and this is what we had been dealing with from the very beginning of our procedure, had any experience with adoption directly from Kenya to the Netherlands. No doubt Kenyan children had been adopted by Dutch parents in the past, but they had eventually travelled to the Netherlands after a longer stay in Kenya. Nobody, not even our friends from Nyumbani, was certain of what we needed. And as for us, at this point we knew absolutely nothing and simply let ourselves be manoeuvred from one authority to the next.

The following day also failed to produce any result on the part of Mr. Odhiambo, but we did receive the *laissez-passer* complete with entry visa from the Dutch embassy. For a small fee (official stamps et cetera) we were able to obtain the papers and, with the help of many obliging, friendly people, take one last photo for the album. Thus we set off with the Dutch papers to Nyumbani. But the people there refused to believe that this was all we needed, and they did not allow us to take Mette. A day later, we had another appointment with Mr. Odhiambo and we decided to take Mette with us. Close to tears, we set off again. And this time, a miracle happened. We engaged in conversation about children (as we had Mette with us) with another official and we explained our problem once more, explaining to him how Nyumbani and the lawyer were saying we needed identity papers for Mette, a sort of passport, in order to be able to take her out of the country. Despite our exhaustion inside the hot and stuffy building on this eternal afternoon, we told the official a short version of our long story, and were promptly presented with a temporary passport for Mette in the form of a large yellow document with photo and plenty of official stamps. We are sure that it was Mette herself who had made this happen.

There was no time to travel back to Nyumbani to say our good-byes properly. We wanted to get home as soon as possible. The plane was due to leave at eight in the evening. We had food and drink for Mette. For the first time it was just the three of us, and we went back to our hotel room two blocks away. We were visited in the nick of time by some beloved Dutch acquaintances who had been very supportive throughout the developments and who wanted one more look at Mette. Little Mette was sleeping peacefully on our big bed as we made our preparations to go home.

26 November 1999

Homecoming

Before we left the hotel, we phoned home to give the family the approximate arrival time. Nice and early for those picking us up: the plane was due to land at six thirty in the morning.

We set off to the airport in an old English taxi well on time. We had the stand-by tickets in our bag but were apprehensive about the seats and above all, customs. No matter how insistently we had been told that everything was now under control, the last few days were still so fresh in our minds that only seeing was believing. We had agreed to first show only the Dutch *laissez-passer*. We were confident about the information we had obtained from the embassy. If that should prove insufficient, we could then always bring out Mette's big yellow identity paper.

But all went well. Waved off by an enthusiastic ground team (we also knew them well after so many years of their moral support), we passed effortlessly through customs and were given a window seat, Mette was on my lap. We were on our way home.

What I remember most about the flight was the absence of a strong, overwhelming feeling of relief. Everything seemed to be normal; a sleeping child on my lap, a buggy in the luggage compartment, a nappy change in the toilet. We ourselves hardly slept at all of course, but the ultimate feeling of relief and the accompanying tears failed to come. Of course we were happy, but not euphoric. It later occurred to me that it has to stop at some point, tears are used up and after a certain period of time one cannot or will not feel tension anymore.

The landing at Amsterdam Schiphol Airport was like coming home; our crusade was almost at an end. To our surprise, a befriended colleague was standing at the gate, also well informed about our arrival day, to welcome us with balloons. Mette was unperturbed by all the excitement.

She loved the balloons but she was very tired. The crew, who had spoilt us throughout the flight, waved us off, and the four of us headed for customs. After another short moment of tension at customs we were congratulated and were through. All papers were in order!

At baggage collection we could already see the big banner: "Welcome Mette!" The baggage seemed to take an eternity to show up, and the tears started flowing as soon as we caught of sight family and friends. It was real, not a dream, we had come home with our daughter. Everyone was congratulating us and admiring Mette, and the crew room was laid out with the famous biscuits and aniseed sprinkles, as well as presents for Mette. Writser's mother saw her granddaughter for the first time, as did other uncles, aunts and our dear friends. I must say: Mette was wonderful, remaining calm throughout fuss, but at some point she was simply too tired. Writser went to fetch the car (equipped with baby seat!) from the staff car park and everyone went their separate ways, to different corners of the country. We would not be seeing them again for a while, as we had agreed to first give Mette time to get used to us and to her new home.

As soon as we were in the car, Mette fell into a deep sleep from which she would only awaken much later. We drove home knowing that my parents would be waiting in our house as my father was not well enough to wait at the airport for hours.

No words can describe our amazement as we drove along the main road on which we live. The section leading up to our house was decorated with flags and pink balloons. The neighbours had all hung out their flags, and our next door neighbours were standing outside our house waiting to meet us. Such warm feelings! They discreetly withdrew to their own houses after the initial greeting, and we entered our balloon-clad house. Tiny Mette had slept through everything. It had just turned eight o'clock. My father's expression is immortalized on video, his emotion and awe at the little bundle sleeping happily in my mother's arms. Mette slowly woke up, crept around on the carpet in the living room and started to cry. Maybe she had a dirty nappy or was just a little afraid, so I picked her up and held her close to me, but all in vain. Looking back, I think it was my mother who suggested she might be hungry. Writser, who also has a good appetite, could well understand that and raced off to the supermarket to get some baby rice, for we hadn't organised any supplies yet. There was no food in the house for Mette to eat. The baby rice arrived and the bowl was soon empty – she could certainly eat – and the big day, her first day on Dutch soil, could begin.

The house was filled with flowers and festive feelings. Two baby hampers were waiting in the living room for mother and baby. It was like a dream, yet it was true. We had given birth and at last Mette had arrived, at last we could celebrate.

Later that day we went to the printer's to arrange the "new arrival" cards.

no words
can express
how we have longed for you
and how welcome you are

still hard to believe
a miracle
a child
for us
to travel with us

On the day of our arrival in the Netherlands we received an e-mail from Nyumbani:

> *Congratulations and welcome to Holland. We hope all went well at both airports. All of us wish you congratulations and say Bravo!! Mette has a new home.*
> *Mom Margareth sends her regards and she reminds me to let you know that Mette likes rice porridge and mashed potatoes.*
> *We wish you all the best and keep us informed about you all.*
> *Protus.*

From my diary

28 November
It's five o'clock and you're playing happily in your play pen. You've just had a nap, because you were tired after our walk with your pram.

Everything went smoothly on the first night in your new cot and new house. We put your cot next to our double bed so as not to miss anything. At four o'clock you were awake briefly, but after we had pulled the cord of your beloved jumping jack, you went back to sleep till half past six. Daddy and mummy were also well awake by then as we had gone to bed very early the night before. We were tired from all the emotions. We took you into bed with us and gave you a big bowl of baby rice. What an appetite! Even daddy was impressed. Another novelty after breakfast: the big bathtub. You went in with mummy and although you were a little unsure at first, you soon loved it. Daddy dried you and got you dressed and at half past eight you fell asleep downstairs in your play pen. An hour later you woke up again and waved mummy off to church. The minister told the wonderful story of your arrival. When mummy came home from church, you had fallen asleep again, this time on daddy's tummy. An endearing sight.

Your first sandwich went down without a problem. With renewed energy we explored a new world, your world. We had bought you a thick ski suit so you wouldn't get cold. We saw a lot of familiar faces while we were out and all were unanimous in their opinion: a gorgeous child.

You enjoyed the walk and looked around you with amazement. You were wearing your hat with cords and real mittens. Of course our walk took us to the petting zoo and now you are back in your play pen as we relax on the couch. It is still so unreal. Father, mother, child. We can't take our eyes off you; our days are filled with you. A child; our child.

29 November
A busy day, so we won't have a bath, it makes you quite tired... You slept all the way through to half past seven! That was wonderful, although it doesn't mean that we also slept well. We heard every tiny sound and had to put the light on to make sure you were comfortable. Daddy gives you a quick wash and we have some breakfast after you've polished off a big plate of baby rice and a bottle of milk. It is high time we ordered the cards – your arrival cards. We go for a nice walk as the weather is lovely. Again we see plenty of familiar faces and you chuckle happily. We buy stamps, make an appointment at town hall and when we get home we phone the aliens police, both to register you. You are doing so well, high-spirited, playing with books in your play pen, crawling around investigating every corner and babbling baby talk.

In the afternoon, we visit the doctor, who is also undoubtedly impressed by your charming appearance. He examines your eyes, which seem to be a little lazy. He also looks at the patch on your head and gives us some ointment to put on it. We'll have to make an appointment at the hospital for a full check-up, but there's no hurry.

Tonight we are having cauliflower and chicken, you eat it all up and still have room for a bottle of milk. To our surprise you still have the energy to play in your pen for another hour before sleep gets the better of you.

10 December

Yesterday you were at the hospital and the doctor found you to be in excellent health. As a reward you were given two injections, which have left you a little poorly today. Apart from that, you are doing wonderfully. Grandpa and grandma have seen you a few times now. Grandpa's thrilled to bits with you. He was a little worried before you came to the Netherlands that it would not feel the same with a child who was no flesh and blood of one of his children. But nothing could be further from the truth. You are so sweet he could eat you up as you sit there on his lap. You've already read the newspaper with him today, you are very peaceful when you sit with him. You certainly know where you belong. We think it is because we knew each other so long before you came here. You already knew our smell, the sound of our voices, our warmth, and this familiarity shows in your behaviour. It is as if this is how it should always have been.

Tonight you slept in your own room for the first time. Not so cosy, but mummy and daddy hadn't slept a wink with all the little noises you make at night. But you slept through easily and although the door was open we did not hear you at all. You are also making progress in Dutch. You already know every word to two Dutch children's songs. You crawl across the room at top speed and it is a perfect delight to see you go like that. You also love to stand up and walk along pushing your buggy, your little feet all over the place with each step. Today you started drinking out of a sippy cup, ate a rice cake at coffee time and in general are eating us out of house and home.

14 December

The Christmas cards are ready and we've taken the opportunity to tell relatives and friends how well you are doing and how happy we are as a family. The new year will get us on the phone to start arranging for you to meet everyone at last. We think you are up to it now. Everything is a joy with you. I'll post the cards tomorrow, it is too late now.

The night of 14/15 December
Shock

The telephone rings
As we're tucked up in bed
Let it ring…
What time does the alarm go off?

Alright, we'll answer
It's late
But you never know
What it might be about

You should come
Your father's not well
And you get into the car
As you always do

For not well is not so bad
That's just off-colour
That's what I thought on the way
After the alarm clock phone

And I saw my brother
Cheeks wet with tears
And still I thought: don't overreact
But there was no passing it off with a joke

Dad's just unwell
I thought going upstairs
And then I saw
Couldn't believe my eyes
My mother on the phone

And his eyes closed
A cloth around his chin
He hadn't moved

My father was lying very still
I saw a piece of bread from breakfast
I saw my father and I knew
My father is gone.

18 December
Side by side

I play with our child
Clap your hands
I look at her huge eyes and laugh
As a tear falls down my cheek

How strange life is

My father died
Our child had just arrived
A photo of us
One of countless dreams

How mysterious life is
How things go hand in hand
Death and life
So strange, and yet

So remarkably true

2000 begins

The spectacular start to the new millennium passed us by without much ado but with many tears. The excess of emotions in such a short time had made us tired and vulnerable. Mette was our sunshine, a real little baby to warm and cherish us. We often imagined how different things would have been if we were still caught up in all the nightmarish procedures. Perhaps my father, with his tired body, lungs and heart had managed to wait for Mette's arrival before finding the peace of mind to close his eyes for the last time. At the start of January, we decided to go and stay in a holiday park in the Netherlands for a few days to relax and recharge our energy. All packed up, we set off on our first holiday with a child, in a car that was rather over packed for a five-day trip. How we enjoyed the first days. Mette in the buggy, in the swimming pool, on the couch with a baby book, in our big bed in the mornings. It was wonderful, until a stomach flu set in and laid Mette and Writser low. After emptying the umpteenth bucket, we packed up and returned home on Friday morning, more dead than alive. The energy recharge had almost been successful.

Mette was soon on her feet again, but the tension was now manifesting itself physically in Writser. Although he returned to work in January, the company health advisor told me to stay at home for a while to regain strength and emotional balance. This was followed by my winter leave, so I had the chance to be a full-time mother until the end of March. Looking back, this was a blessing. We were unaware of the upheaval that was still to come and it had a healing effect to be able to regain strength after the adoption and the death of my father. It helped me build up reserves for the future.

People often pass comments if you have a child of such obviously different skin colour than your own. The VIA information course had prepared us for this, and it turned out to be true. However, contrary to what the VIA course had predicted, meetings with strangers were always spontaneous and moving. People would say things to us like: "You must be so happy with your child", or: "You look a picture together!" One such occasion occurred in our village when a man with an adopted girl from China came up and spoke to us. We got talking and exchanged experiences. He told us that the Ministry of Justice was applying a new regulation which would enable adoptive parents like ourselves to adopt another young child although we were now both past forty. As Writser was forty-two at that stage and there must be no more than forty years between the age of the elder parent and the age of the child on its arrival in the Netherlands, we would normally only be eligible to adopt a child of two or older. We did not like the idea of Mette then being less than a year older than her sibling, as it would create an imbalance in the family.

Fortunately, the Ministry of Justice recognises this problem and has devised regulations to let natural development of a family prevail. The Netherlands calls this exceptional regulation the 'younger sibling placement regulation'. We were very pleasantly surprised to hear about this provision and decided to call the Ministry of Justice immediately for more information. On February 28, I called the Ministry in The Hague in a state of great excitement. And it was true: thanks to the said regulation, we had the option of adopting a younger child, despite our age. We could hardly believe our luck.

On 3 March, we sent an application to the Ministry of Justice requesting to adopt another foreign child. We knew that by the time we were eligible for a second procedure, Mette would have been living in the Netherlands for a year, but someone had advised us to send the letter nevertheless, as we would then be allocated a BKA number, which indicates that you wish to adopt a foreign child. This number would determine our position on the list of prospective adoptive parents. Of course we received a reply advising us to carefully read the rules governing second-child adoptions and telling us to come back at the end of November, exactly one year after Mette's arrival in the Netherlands. We did not mind, we had been given another BKA number and that marked the start of the procedure. Our next letter would be dropping through their letterbox exactly one year after Mette's arrival, BKA number and all.

Another surprise came in a telephone conversation with a colleague of ours who, together with her husband, was also in the process of trying to adopt from Nyumbani. She visited the orphanage regularly to be with her future daughter and kept us well informed of the goings-on over there. Two children, a boy and a girl, had recently been brought in and would eventually be offered up for adoption. Writser and I exchanged knowing looks and after talking it through sent an e-mail to Nyumbani explaining the new situation. On 10 March, we received the following reply by e-mail:

> "We are pleased to hear that you consider adopting a brother or a sister for Mette from Nyumbani. From our side we will be more than willing to assist you if such a time comes. At the moment we have two babies but neither of them is confirmed negative. There is a boy Stephen, who will be 3 months on the 14th of March and a girl Ann, who is two months now. Perhaps when Geeri comes in April she can meet them. Now we cannot promise you much unless you wait as you did with Mette…"

We were expecting again.

Expecting in 2000

On 22 March, Mette took her first steps.

(She had already seen her first snow and her first snowman and had been on her first journey abroad.) Grandma had joined us on a ten-day skiing trip and all four of us had had a wonderful time.

Right before we set off on holiday, we sent an e-mail to Nyumbani saying we wished to adopt a boy and that I would be coming to Kenya on 10 April to talk to them about it. Of course I would then see our son-to-be and Nyumbani would have to consent to the match.

On 11 April 2000, I set off to Nyumbani once more to meet our son, again with a colleague who wanted to come with me, and again without Writser. This time, however, it was a very conscious decision as one of us had to stay behind to look after Mette. To strengthen the bonding process, we had agreed that Mette should be with one of us as much as possible, so that she could always rely on either her mother or her father to be around. As we both worked part-time, we were able to take turns flying and still have enough time to be together as a family.

After an elaborate welcome at Nyumbani – it was the first time I had been back there since Mette's adoption – and a long conversation about our motives for adopting a second child, why a boy, etc., I was allowed to go and look inside house Claire where Wisse was lying waiting in his cot.

Wisse was almost four months old at the time. He was born on 15 December 1999, a day after my father's death. This felt like a very special date; a guarantee for a perfect match. We were sure this child was meant for us.

A beautiful baby lay in the bed beside the big bed of mama Beatrice, his regular nanny. He had a very light complexion, rather like chocolate brown, and looked as if he needed another coat of paint. At that moment there was no one else in the house and I lifted him out of his cot and held him close to me. It is hard to fathom that you might be holding your child at such a moment. Incredible to realise that from that moment on you are possessed by an unstoppable urge to have him with you always. Uncanny how little time it takes for a picture to become engrained on your retina and locked in your heart forever. The sperm had reached the ovum and was not about to reverse fertilisation. I carried him outside and sat down on an easy chair to savour this new addition to our family, this handsome little man – and what a beautiful baby he was. Soft little curls and a lovely round face which looked so peaceful and content. And so soft. I remember Wisse's softness so well. Bright eyes of a beautiful brown. One little fist in his mouth and the other gripping a soft yellow doll made for him by a very special neighbour undeterred by a serious illness. It was made of soft yellow felt and filled with sheep's wool. At home I had carried it around with me for a few days so that the wool would take on my scent. In this way Wisse, small and so far away though he was, would be able to get used to his mother's scent. I pressed him against my skin and softly sang to him. My thoughts wandered: I could not imagine this radiant baby to be unhealthy. I was pregnant and had been allowed to sneak a look inside my womb.

Much later, after he had fallen asleep, I laid Wisse back in his cot and went back to the hotel to prepare myself for the flight home where Writser was eagerly waiting to hear my account of our first meeting and of course to see the photos and video.

On 15 April we received an e-mail from Nyumbani saying that after consultations with Father d'Agostino, the social worker and the head nurse it had been decided that Wisse would be allocated to us for adoption if he should turn out to be healthy.

Let me explain the phrase 'turn out to be healthy' in a little more detail. As with Mette, HIV antibodies had been detected in Wisse's blood. As explained earlier, this means that our children's mothers, like so many young Kenyans, were infected with the HIV virus. At present, a high proportion of the 18-35 age group is infected with the virus. This does not automatically mean that their children are also infected; only time will tell whether or not they are healthy. It has been found that the majority of these children will rid themselves of these antibodies by means of their own immune system if offered a good home with good food and plenty of love and attention. It takes approximately one year before this can be demonstrated reliably, so children are tested around the age of one to see if their blood still contains antibodies. If there are none, the child is as healthy as any other child. If antibodies are still present the child is also infected with the HIV virus.

Like with Mette, we decided to take the unique opportunity to make the bonding as successful as possible. We would bond with Wisse without knowing whether he would be declared healthy or if the adoption would be successful. We were delighted by the e-mail from Kenya saying he would be allocated to us if he turned out to be healthy. We had another child. We put a photo on the coffee table in the living room, and started to prepare Mette. Look Mette, this is your brother. She was a fast learner. This was Wisse. Although we had kept Mette's name a secret, Wisse's full name in all its glory soon became a part of the family and our circle of friends. To a certain extent this was a risk, for if things did not work out for whatever reason, the whole world would know that we were heartbroken. But did that really matter? Is it not thanks to the support of family and friends that you find the strength to carry on in difficult times? Therefore, we decided to take the risk and Wisse was on display in photos and videos. As a result, everyone felt like they already knew him when he eventually arrived in the Netherlands. In that respect, the element of surprise had been removed, but the future had plenty of other surprises in store.

Easter 2000

We had been spontaneously involved in Mette's baptism, but Wisse's ceremony seemed one from which we would quite definitively be absent. One of the questions we put to Nyumbani was when Wisse was to be baptised. It had already been scheduled for Easter, which meant that we would not be able to be present as we had quite different schedules which were not so easy to rearrange. So we e-mailed back asking if the baptism could take place on another day, fully confident that this would be no problem. But no, that was not possible. I well remember that we were both angry and disappointed. We would not be able to be with him on that special day.

Wisse's baptism (he was still called Stephen at the time, but we already considered him our child), was to be part of the Easter ceremony. I consider myself an open-minded person, but did not understand why out of all the children in Nyumbani they could not choose a different one. We never managed to see eye to eye with the people from Nyumbani on this matter, although there was no lack of goodwill. We were allowed to pass on the names we wanted for his baptism, so we gave the subject careful thought. Writser wanted to keep his own name in the family, which was also the name of his grandfather. I thought it a wonderful idea, as long as we would call him by a different name for practical reasons. We used name books to eventually choose Wisse, which means 'good'. And that is how it felt: good. So his first name would bear reference to Writser's roots. His second name we chose after my paternal grandfather, who had actually been registered with an incorrect name: he should have been called Ietsen, but the registrar had turned it into IJsen, which went unnoticed for many years. When the mistake was finally discovered, it was too late to change it, so IJsen it was for the rest of his life. IJsen was Metje's husband, which brought Mette and Wisse closer together through their names. Wisse's last name would be Stephen, the name he had been given in Nyumbani. His initials would then spell WIJS – Dutch for "wise" – which we thought rather special. We only found out later that the name Stephen came from a rich Italian woman who had lost her own son Stephen in an accident. She had donated a large sum of money to the church and requested that a child be given the name Stephen after her son. When we heard this story we no longer felt comfortable with the name. We understood that this mother could not let go of her dead child, but did not like the idea of her feeling of sadness being passed on to our future child. It seemed inappropriate that he should go through life with such a stigma.

But the baptism took place in our absence. Probably, though we will never know for sure, Wisse was indeed baptised with the name Stephen, although we no longer agreed with this name. (Incidentally, he was discharged from hospital with the name: baby Grace Muthoni.) We were angry because no one had listened to us, yet we did not want to be angry because Nyumbani had done so much for us, and we were sad because we could not be present at such a beautiful moment in our lives.

After talking with Nyumbani, we finally decided on the names Writser IJsen Muthoni, the last name in honour of Wisse's biological mother. And that is what it now says on the baptism certificate, albeit with tipp-ex.

More in 2000

We were frequent guests in Nyumbani all through that year. Wisse was constantly cuddled and filmed from all angles – front and back, from the side, above and below. He was completely different from Mette. For one, Mette had been much smaller than Wisse. Wisse weighed almost six pounds at birth – quite a different story from three-pound Mette. While Mette enchanted everyone with her huge eyes, Wisse did so with his cheeky and entertaining manner. Apart from the fact that he frequently suffered from colds and coughed a lot, he too turned out healthy and we had high hopes that everything would work out fine. We took it in turns to visit him twice a month. Mette was in the safe hands of the other one of us at those times and able to stay in her familiar surroundings. The arrangement suited all of us very well.

As we were busy to-ing and fro-ing to see Wisse, we were also thoroughly enjoying life with Mette. She was a wonderful child. She loved going to toddlers' swimming lessons and enjoyed the company of people. She was at times very independent and at the end of autumn came her second birthday, which meant she could start pre-school. That would certainly be no trouble given her social skills. We bought a big tent for next year's family holiday, and November came.

On 8 November, almost a year after Mette had arrived in the Netherlands, we were scheduled to work together on a flight to Nairobi. My mother looked after Mette as we enjoyed our journey. We had always liked working together and as we had had to do without it for some time it was all the more special. The following morning we went to see the lawyer.

We had been allocated a different lawyer this time, but had not really been satisfied with her so far. We had become so attached to Esther, our lawyer in Mette's adoption process, and did not know what to do about Justine. She was absolutely never on time, seemed to be constantly preoccupied with other matters and showed no real determination to bring our adoption to a successful close. Several things had changed in Kenya over the past year. In August, a case of child smuggling had come to light, which was bad news for foreign adoptions in general. Judges were even more alert to foreigners coming to adopt a child and Justine clearly found it an uncomfortable situation. She held a high position at the court and did not want to get burned. All in all, communications with her were exhausting and caused much irritation and hence also stress on our part. Nyumbani did not do any better with her, although they certainly tried; they had, for example, invited her to join the board of directors so that she could be more involved in the welfare of Nyumbani's children.

For most of that Thursday morning, we merely sat outside her office feeling annoyed. Now wizened to the procedure, we had brought along books, food, and drink to help while away the waiting time. After a serious conversation during which Justine emphasised that we could not take a second adoption for granted, we set off for Nyumbani. We had told Justine that although the procedure had not become any easier, we wanted to fight to the end. That meant right up to the court case and the judge's final decision. We had quite definitely 'hired' her.

Visiting Wisse together was quite an experience. The dear little boy was now almost a year old and incredibly active; he could almost walk on his own. It was so wonderful to be able to share these moments – to play together, eat together, go for walks together – just like a normal family.

We had also had talks about Wisse's blood test. Mette had been tested very early, and Wisse did not seem any less healthy and we were very eager to find out the result. Nyumbani promised that they would attend to the matter as they now had access to their own laboratory, which meant they could perform the test themselves. Altogether it would take until January 2001. We had made plenty of enquiries into the situation on our visits and in e-mails and did not understand what was taking so long. Wisse was barely ever sick, aside from the occasional cold or cough. It was only much later that the cat was let out of the bag in a conversation with Nyumbani's doctor. Their own laboratory was missing a certain reagent, a laboratory substance necessary for the test. It was difficult for them to admit to white people that something was not possible, and so they tried to keep us hanging avoiding having to tell us that they were not actually able to perform the test. They were afraid to lose face. And after all those years we thought that they saw us as equals.

That conversation with the doctor took place on 11 January, and the decision was made to take a sample of Wisse's blood, prepare it for transport and take it to the Netherlands so that Writser could deliver it to the hospital the next day. It was the egg of Columbus. We still had to see whether the Dutch hospital would accept to do it. After some negotiation, the hospital consented. The sticking point was that the hospital had no proof that the blood was definitely Wisse's. Of course they had a point. They eventually took our word for it and performed the test. We would receive the result later in January. We were starting to feel somewhat uneasy, because everything was taking so much longer than with Mette. In our hearts we could not conceive of the fact that the news would be bad, but we would have no real peace of mind until we had received the all-clear.

We returned from our journey with more stories for Mette, more photos and videos.

Two days later we celebrated Mette's second birthday in a big way – it was her first birthday in the Netherlands. Everyone was invited and Mette was in her element. There were lots of cakes and kisses, people and presents. A few days later, she was to start pre-school, and she needed no encouragement to go. She was, and still is, most welcome. The excitement, the boyfriends and girlfriends, the scissors, glue, paint, sing-alongs and stories, Mette loved it all, and still thoroughly enjoys these activities.

The year before, we had celebrated her birthday in Nyumbani. This time, we celebrated in our own home. So much had changed over the past year. The stress from the adoption, bringing Mette to the Netherlands, my father's death and the recovery period. All that followed closely and unexpectedly by the procedures of the new addition to our family who had to stay in Kenya until his time came to be picked up. If all went according to plan…

27 November - 27 January

All year we had waited patiently for 27 November, Mette's day of arrival in the Netherlands, which was now exactly one year ago. Until that day, we could do little more than wait. It is actually wise to avoid creating too much unnecessary work for yourself. You need time to get used to the adopted child and the new situation of parenthood, but in our case the fact that Wisse had so clearly bonded with us over a period of almost eight months, nearly a pregnancy, complicated the situation. However, we had prepared ourselves for that and accepted the way it was to be. We were in touch with the Africa Foundation and the Child Protection Agency over the phone about the procedures we had to follow. We were open and honest to them about the situation and received full cooperation from the Netherlands in order to move things along as quickly as possible. We were thus granted a very early interview with the Child Protection Agency, which was to take place in our home. We had requested that the interview be conducted by the same woman we had spoken to about Mette, and we were relieved to hear that in fact that was standard policy. Little explanation was needed and she saw with her own eyes how Mette felt totally at home in her new surroundings. The resulting report would again be sent to the Ministry of Justice and the Africa Foundation, after which we would be granted a new "consent in principle". Later in the proceedings, we did in fact receive a copy of this report, as the Kenyan Child Protection Agency needed it, and it is now stored carefully in the file we have on the two children as a souvenir for the future.

We also submitted the medical certificate and the certificate of good conduct, but ultimately, the paperwork from the Netherlands was less voluminous than before. It was, after all, our second adoption, we thought rather arrogantly. That should make things easier. The contact address (Nyumbani) in Kenya was the same and thus already checked, now needing only an update. Communication from the Ministry of Justice was fast and efficient and on 28 November, we received an encouraging letter announcing that procedures were underway.

In Kenya, however, it was evident that far less was under way. In view of the child trafficking I mentioned earlier, the general attitude towards foreign adoptions was not particularly positive. Furthermore, there was no hurrying the lawyer along and we were still none the wiser about Wisse's health. Such was the state of affairs at the end of 2000.

Normally, adopting is not too much of a problem in Kenya. If you live there and can prove that you have looked after the child for three months and (needless to say) the child has no family, or none which can look after it, adoption proceedings may be initiated and there will generally not be too many problems. Things only become more complicated, if one has not lived in Kenya for the three obligatory months, yet wants to adopt. Our line of approach was to have the total of our individual visits considered as equalling the compulsory three months. This formula had worked when we adopted Mette, but this time it could prove more difficult.

So things were not going too well in Kenya; in fact, they were going decidedly badly. By now we had worn down the step to the lawyer's practice with our frequent visits (we were there at least every other week), and each time there was something else to delay the procedure. On top of it all, we got the feeling that our lawyer was not particularly concerned with our case. We realised how we had been spoilt with Esther and now missed her terribly. It was a source of great stress to us.

Meanwhile, Wisse had his first birthday, which we celebrated in Kenya with all the trimmings. Wisse himself had a surprise for us: he could walk. In just two weeks time, he had taken the chance to learn. We watched his progress with mixed feelings: his world had suddenly become so much bigger, and although I was happy for him, I also realised that we had experienced all those phases with Mette at home in the Netherlands. We had seen this new development too, but from a distance. He also seemed to have grown. Sometimes the feeling came over us that we were missing out on his development. On the other hand, we felt that we should not complain. After all, most adoptive parents were far less fortunate than we were and generally did not see their child until its pick-up in the country of origin, or sometimes not even until its arrival at Schiphol Airport. But being only human, at times we really had to fight off our own impatience. You might even say it that was partly our own fault, as we had started to believe that Wisse would become our child as early as April.

Early in December, we were visited by a couple who also wanted to adopt children from Kenya. We told them about our experiences and it seemed that a proper little community of Kenyan children was set to come to the Netherlands. The other girl from Nyumbani had already arrived in August, so there were now two children from Kenya here, and two more probably on the way. This was a very encouraging development.

December came. The report from the Child Protection Agency arrived just before Christmas, together with a promise that the remaining outstanding points would be concluded at the start of January. This indeed happened. On 8 January, we had the consent in principle, and the corks were soon popping again.

This also made us double the pressure on the Kenyan lawyer. We made sure all the forms were in order, now including the consent principle, and considering how we had conducted Mette's procedure, it was time to send our application for the adoption of Wisse to the Kenyan court.

Writser celebrated New Year's Eve with Wisse in Kenya while I stayed in the Netherlands and went to my godmother's with Mette and my mother. My godmother lived near the other couple who had adopted a child from Nyumbani. When Writser came back from Kenya we went to see them in the town of Deventer the next day, so we could catch up on each other's news. It was a wonderful feeling to be in the same position as someone else. There was nothing like a fellow-sufferer to really understand the frustrating things about Kenya as a country to adopt from. No one to understand better how you feel, how uncertain all the procedures can make you, even the ones in the Netherlands. And the bliss of flying home with the new family addition – no one else to know that feeling like others who had experienced it. It was a very special evening.

All our working flights in January were destined for Nairobi. We were there every week, so we were able to kill two birds with one stone: we could enjoy seeing Wisse on a weekly basis and giving him a feeling of being at home with his family, and at the same time, we could keep pressing the lawyer. Needless to say, this situation took its toll on domestic life back in the Netherlands, but luckily, there were some pleasant moments of distraction such as a reunion with the VIA course members and an Oleta Adams concert at Amsterdam's legendary Carré theatre.

On 26 January, we took Mette for her final check-up at the hospital. When you enter the Netherlands with an adopted child, a whole lot of procedures are in store for you. You have to go to the aliens police, to the town hall, to the GP and the hospital. There is a special protocol for these children, which involves testing their blood for almost everything. Lungs and wrists are X-rayed, bone development is compared with the standard average for certain ages, et cetera. The Dutch Ministry of Health requires that children regularly visit a so-called "consultation office" to see a children's nurse whose responsibilities include monitoring the child's health and administering vaccinations.

Mette's first check-up had already shown her to be healthy. As her vitamin D level was rather low, she was given supplements. The worst thing was that it was difficult to get blood samples from Mette. For the first one, they needed quite a lot of blood, and she cried so much that she almost fell asleep from exhaustion. Finally, after almost three quarters of an hour, veins and fingertips bloody, enough blood had been extracted to fill the tubes. As an ex-nurse, I mistakenly thought I was hardened to such scenes, but I ended up crying as uncontrollably as Mette, feeling so powerless. But there was also good news. On this memorable day we received news that Wisse was healthy. Mette did not need a return visit either; we were now blessed with two healthy children. We thanked the doctor and hoped to see her again soon with child number two. Another reason to celebrate!

28 January - 21 March

The first post of the year came from the Africa Foundation. On 29 January, we received confirmation that the application for the entry visa had been sent to the IND (Immigration and Naturalisation Department). This was wonderful news. We had paid another administration fee of 680 euros, which included the cost of verifying the contact details of the orphanage, and were overall satisfied with the Dutch adoption apparatus. Kenya, however, had less good news to offer. Our 'enthusiastic' lawyer sent us an e-mail on 19 February saying the following:

> *"Due to the strict practice now being applied by the high court in Kenya, the chances of your adoption application succeeding are very low... Nonetheless and being mindful of and understanding the above restrictions to your application, could you please inform us whether you still wish to proceed with the adoption application and are prepared to pay our non-refundable legal fees".*

In the same e-mail she informed us that due to the stricter procedures now being applied in Kenya, we would be having an interview with the Child Protection Agency in Kenya. For this purpose, the report from the Dutch Child Protection Agency had to be translated and sent to Kenya. Fortunately, a friend of ours (who happened to be a translator) offered to do this for us. With his help we were able to honour our lawyer's request, even if we were rather affronted that she, of all people, should use the word 'immediately'.

Meanwhile, the following happened in Kenya. On 23 February, the first step was due to be taken towards starting court proceedings for the adoption. Prior to the actual adoption, a temporary guardian is appointed while the court case is under way, as was the procedure with Mette. This absolves the orphanage of its responsibility as carer, which is passed on to the temporary guardian. This process involves taking note of all the credentials of the adoptive parents, and this legal procedure is seen as precursor to the final adoption procedure. In Mette's case, we had asked Nicolas to be temporary guardian, and now for Wisse we asked Protus, the manager of the orphanage. Protus was on his way to priesthood and was a man of great integrity who had always been close to us. By asking him we wanted to show our gratitude as we had done for Mette's adoption case by asking Nicolas. Approval was granted for Protus to be appointed temporary guardian, and the final court hearing was scheduled for 23 March. It was a time to rejoice, but there was also tension.

Mette's papers gave us less cause for rejoicing.

One year after the adoptive child's arrival, one may start proceedings to adopt the child according to Dutch law, whereby the child is granted the Dutch nationality and is allowed a Dutch passport. Until then, the child has a foreign status. So when the child arrives, one has to go to the aliens police, which marks the start of the procedure. We had done all of this for Mette. We had then applied for guardianship under Dutch law, as we were still only guardians under Kenyan law, and on 27 November had started the procedure for Dutch citizenship. A good friend of ours is a lawyer and was glad to be of help. We ourselves were not fully aware of the fact that although you do indeed apply for Dutch citizenship for the child, an "intention to adopt" has to be filed, which entails another three months of waiting before the child actually takes the Dutch nationality and may be registered in a passport, even after the approval of citizenship by the judge. These three months are intended to give third parties the opportunity to object to the adoption under Dutch law. It is similar to the procedure of filing an "intention to marry" and an equally ridiculous formality. We were nevertheless very worried about the situation. Due to the December holidays, the legal team were in no hurry to speed up the paperwork, and although our friend did her utmost to move things along, they were not moving fast enough. On 14 February (indeed!), we received the judge's approval for Mette's naturalisation, but our joy was immediately suppressed when an unwitting clerk in our village explained the rest of the procedure to us (regarding the three months' waiting period). I sat sobbing in the same room where we had announced our intention to marry. It was now March, the court case in Kenya was due to start, and of course we wanted to take Mette with us as we did not know how long we would have to stay there this time. We would have to combine our holiday with the ten days' adoption leave, but this would only be possible if Mette could go with us. And without papers, Mette would not be able to come, but we could not leave her behind in the Netherlands for an indefinite period of time. Stress was building up again.

We were on a wild goose chase. We phoned the embassy in Kenya, who told us they could not issue anything that would solve our problem. On 14 March, we went to The Hague again to talk to the people from the embassy in person. We had all the documents from the foreign police with us, as well as the papers we had got from the Kenyan authorities before leaving Kenya with Mette. We were shown into a large waiting room where people soon started talking to us. People in Kenya are generally very open and friendly, and the Kenyans at the embassy were no different. They were most interested in our adoptive child who, of course, was on her very best behaviour. She enchanted them all. Once our turn came to explain our predicament to a specialist, it took no time at all. The paper we had been given in Kenya before Mette's departure and which had been so difficult to obtain turned out to be an official temporary Kenyan passport on which Mette could leave and enter the country freely for two years. So we could travel with her to Kenya without any problems. We had been sitting on a pearl at home, and never even realised it! We were over the moon returning home to continue our travel preparations.

I am getting ahead of things a little, because Writser and I first had to be present in Nairobi. They were busy days, but it seemed to all be working out. Writser had been in Nairobi on 26 February, and came back with the request that we come for an appointment on 9 March with Karen Kaninu, a social worker who would talk us through the preparation of the court case. Luckily, we had received the translated report on 4 March and both had weekly flights to Nairobi, so together we set off to Kenya on stand-by tickets on Thursday 8 March in between duty flights. Writser had returned from Nairobi that morning at six o'clock, so he could easily be at Schiphol airport again at 9 to fly back to where he had just come from (sometimes it is best to try not to think about what you are doing to yourself). Fortunately, there were seats available (another additional stress factor, but one cannot turn down the opportunity of such low fares), Writser could sleep on the outward journey and I enjoyed the attention we were given by our colleagues in my own small way. Everyone was extremely sympathetic and offered their very best wishes. We had booked a night in the hotel where the crew was staying, and we were to fly back with them the next evening. I had to work the following Sunday – on a flight to, where else, Nairobi. First, we had an appointment with the lawyer on Friday morning, after which we would go visit Wisse in Nyumbani. There, we would also meet Karen. We were quite curious. We had been given to understand that a lot would depend on her report. How would she view the fact that we had built up a bond with Wisse but had not lived with him in Kenya for the three months required to take care of him? We would soon find out. And then there was the question of whether her report would be ready in time for the court case. The average bureaucratic speed in Kenya was slower than in the Netherlands, which added yet another aspect of uncertainty. The proceedings were due to start in two weeks.

We met in Protus's office. We had already picked up Wisse and were playing with him happily. To cut a long story short, it was nowhere near as bad as we had feared. Karen was very friendly, had a wonderful sense of humour and put us at ease immediately. She promised to have the report ready on time and ask Justine to present things as positively as possible. Much later we were able to read the report and it contained nothing but praise. What was striking were the details of our possessions. By Kenyan standards we are of course extremely rich and that is how the report read. It is true that we do not live in a hut out in a field somewhere, but when you look at our circumstances through the eyes of a Kenyan, it puts everything into a whole new perspective. Wisse also did his very best to make a good impression.

Karen writes:

> *"They are already attached to each other. I noticed this when I visited Nyumbani with them. The infant quickly went to them and would not allow any other person to touch him…"*

We went home already feeling victorious.

21 March - 23 March

We spent these few days attending to the final arrangements before our journey to Kenya. We had the arrival cards designed along the same lines as Mette's, only the details for Wisse were different. We had to organise our visa and travel documents, prepare the injections for Mette and say goodbye to the family, including my brother and sister-in-law who had just had their second baby, and of course Grandma Anne who played such an important role in Mette's life. With two buggies and in the best of spirits, we set off for Schiphol airport. The journey to Kenya was perfect. Mette behaved wonderfully in business class and we arrived in Nairobi feeling quite relaxed. The first morning was for Nyumbani. The three of us were picked up to take Mette to meet Wisse for the first time. Mette was fascinated and found it all most exciting. Once we were in Nyumbani, things went smoothly. Mette gave Wisse a first kiss and said: "This is my little brother" and that was that. She enjoyed herself tremendously all morning, playing with the older children in the middle of the big playground. She did not recognise her former nanny at first, but warmed to her after a little while. It is extraordinary how children experience these things; she had only been away one and a half years, yet had forgotten everything, not even the smell seemed to come back. We could hardly believe it. Of course we took photos of the first meeting and went back to the hotel that day feeling confident. Wisse was to stay in Nyumbani that night.

The next morning, we would be at the lawyer's at eight o'clock to finalise everything. Nicolas would bring Wisse over from Nyumbani, so that we could all be ready and waiting in the court building to be called in when it was our turn. We attracted a lot of attention walking from the lawyer's office to the court with two buggies and two beautiful black children. We were proud as peacocks. We did not have to wait long to be called into the familiar room where we sat down on the bench at the side. This time, we faced a woman judge. The huge man was not there; this lady had been employed specially for family matters. Justine sat opposite her and again we could hardly understand what was being said. It certainly looked as if Justine did not have much to say. And once again the final ruling barely reached my ears.

This time, however, it was not positive. The judge's ruling was negative. I was floored – or rather, we both were. We stood on the step in front of the court and simply could not believe what had just happened. It was not to be. We just looked at each other incredulously, totally numb. It was like being punched in the face but not feeling the blow until later. We felt nothing. Justine was her usual blasé self, saying: "I did warn you." This was neither understanding nor comforting. We could not even cry. I can still see us standing there as foreigners in a strange city, with no idea where we should go or what we should do next. The strange thing was that, as we drilled Justine with questions, the bottleneck was not the question of the three compulsory months in Kenya but rather the fact that we had made no arrangements for a follow-up programme, which had never been mentioned in Mette's adoption case and so of course we had not prepared in Wisse's case, either. The programme consisted of writing a report every three months. It had to be monitored by the Africa Foundation, and they were far away in the Netherlands. They worked with volunteers and were therefore often unable to operate at short notice. We felt the odds stacked against us. For all we knew, the Foundation would have to convene a meeting to come to a decision (after all, it would be the first time that they were confronted with yet another new procedure), which would mean that we would have to return to the Netherlands. And we had Wisse with us sitting in his buggy, where he looked wonderful, so we were not about to have him taken out of it. We got back into the boxing ring.

At half past ten, we were standing outside again, and we phoned the Africa Foundation straight away. Luckily, we were able to reach them and explained our problem. Of course, they told us that it would not be easy, although they ran a similar programme in Ethiopia. We indicated that that programme would probably be fine as long as it was a follow-up programme, and could they please fax us the details. We were as good as on our knees begging them. Karen, an unexpected source of support and comfort, put in one final supreme effort to indicate the urgency of the matter, and even Justine did her best. Upon our request, they informed the Africa Foundation by fax that it was of the utmost importance for this adoption that they send a report confirming that we were participating in a follow-up programme whereby the Foundation acted as an intermediary and counsellor. Today was wasted, though. This chance was gone and we would have to await a new hearing. Justine would file another application for the following week. After that, the court would go into recess for Easter. Justine did not seem hopeful, but we had got used to that over the past year. We ourselves remained unwavering in our belief that anything was possible.

We had to talk with the staff at Nyumbani because we wanted to take Wisse with us to stay with acquaintances from the next day. It was not easy to arrange. We had to persuade them and then sign a special form saying Nyumbani approved of our taking Wisse. We returned to the hotel exhausted. Fortunately, Mette and Wisse seemed oblivious to our precarious situation and played happily in the huge sandpit by the swimming pool. But we knew. We were totally and utterly despondent. That only changed late in the evening when we received an unexpected fax from the Africa Foundation confirming our participation in the follow-up programme as we had requested. A glimmer of hope returned.

That evening, the four of us were sitting outside having dinner at a restaurant. The weather was beautiful and we should have thoroughly enjoyed all the attention we received, especially from the hotel staff, who had known us for so long and knew all about our mission. They thought it was a wonderful sight to see, but we could barely hold back our tears. Later we sat in our hotel room together before giving the children a bath. This, too, should have been a great celebration, but we were too worried to be able to enjoy it. We were getting paranoid about what would go wrong next. Wisse was walking a little strangely (it was the first time we saw his little bare body as he walked) and we immediately feared that he might have a dislocated hip. We felt anxious and vulnerable. How we had been looking forward to this first evening together in this room with its two cots, but now that the time had come, everything was clouded with doubt and question marks. The fax from the Netherlands gave us reason to be grateful – they must have set to work on our case instantly. Finally, everyone fell asleep, exhausted from the impressions and emotions of the day. Writser and I aware of the blessed sounds of two sleeping children: one our own and one not quite.

23 March - 30 March

The next morning, we packed our cases again and were picked up by Dick, an acquaintance we had known for years from the work we did for his orphanage. He had offered to let us stay at his house and we had gratefully accepted this while we were still in the Netherlands. We had been guests in his house many times before, when he was still married to his first wife, and we were looking forward to a domestic environment in which to relax. But we had misjudged the situation. For one, there was the new house. Dick had recently moved house with his new wife and we had not realised that the new house was much smaller. Our whole family had to sleep in the living room. This involved rearranging the living room every evening, we had a sofa bed, Wisse slept in the camping cot we had brought, and two chairs were pushed together for Mette. Mosquito nets were everywhere, the whole situation was awkward. On top of all that, some fifteen German shepherd dogs ran around freely in the huge garden and terrified Mette. They fouled the whole area, making the garden unsuitable for our adventurous twosome to play in. There was a girl Mette's age for her to play with, Michelle, which was nice, for when Michelle returned from school they had great fun together. But Mette was hardly having a good time. She was tense and it was difficult for us to hide our own sense of unease from the children, although we tried. When we looked back on the ordeal, we agreed that it would have benefited our privacy to have checked into a nearby hotel. We would certainly have had more peace and space to ourselves. But it transpired later that we were in a state of total shock after the judge's negative ruling and were feeling the stress of not knowing whether the second attempt would be successful. Although privacy would certainly have been very valuable, we did feel the healing effect of living with our hosts and being able to share our feelings with them. Still, the lack of privacy took its toll on our already brittle energy. A great advantage was having Internet access, which enabled us to keep in touch with relatives and friends in the Netherlands. We had made a long list of addresses before we left and now e-mailed everyone regularly. Three cheers for e-mail! Here are some excerpts from what we wrote:

25 March, 07.21 hours
Subject: Adopting is no fun.
…This Friday we're due to go back to the court and we hope that the papers will prove to be complete. If not, it all seems quite hopeless. Things aren't looking too good for Mette. She hardly eats, sleeps very badly and this is all connected with the changes, not with Wisse's situation. They're very happy playing together. We're not in top shape ourselves either, of course, worn out is probably the best description, but we're hanging in there until Friday…

25 March, 17.07 hours
We're already well into Sunday, I don't know where the time goes. We seem to have found some sort of peace again at last, insofar as possible. Mette is a little better. She was driving us mad, but what can you do? She's had afternoon naps again and has started to get her appetite back. She has found a great friend in Michelle and they love playing with water in the sun. Yesterday evening it rained heavily and dark clouds are gathering again now. Hopefully, that will bring the temperature down a little. It's very hot inside the house. We sleep under a mosquito net, which also keeps the heat in. We don't sleep too close together, as we sweat so much. We talk about last Friday a lot, as well as the coming Friday, and are hoping for the best. Wisse's getting along wonderfully, a fact that should not be ignored. He seems to have bonded perfectly and he's very funny and clever.

26 March, 18.24 hours
Today was a day of tension and relief. Tension from the fact that we don't see eye to eye with our lawyer here and are still waiting for a new date for the court hearing. Justine appears to be too busy on Friday which means we would have to wait much longer. Writser's climbing the walls. He's phoned

at least six times today to try and speak to her but had no luck. Tomorrow at eight o'clock we'll be on the phone again. We'll phone Nyumbani too to ask if they can speed things up at all or exert any influence on our friend. Mette's doing a little better. She's been having severe nosebleeds. This morning it was so bad that Writser said he would fly home with her if it didn't get any better. It is certainly connected with her crying, because the stronger her emotions are, the heavier the nosebleeds. Mette gives Wisse kisses and attempts to blow-dry his hair. Today she's had a little more to eat. Wisse is a comical little chap and he certainly manages to cope with whatever comes his way. He has an enormous appetite, we can hardly meet his needs. Today beans with mashed potatoes and vanilla pudding for dessert.

Mette particularly enjoyed the shopping today. So did we actually, we were out of the house doing something together as family. Dick had some business to attend to, so we had time to ourselves. We have already optimistically had passport size photos made for Wisse, just in case. We were able to get money out of a machine, and a bakery I know from years ago actually sold breadsticks, which made Mette's day. This evening was the first time that the children did not make a fuss at bedtime, so we were not forced to go to bed at the same time as them, half past eight, in a room dark as night. Instead, we could actually read for a while. The little things can make you really happy sometimes. All we have to deal with now is that awful lawyer. If only we knew a date, we would have something to look forward to. Keep your fingers crossed that we'll have one tomorrow – we'll keep you informed. Dear Mum, don't worry more than we do. There's no point. Somehow we still feel optimistic and even if things get tense now and again, we still hope it'll all turn out well. Till the next e-mail.

27 March, 19.48 hours

Why are you not e-mailing? Good news today. Nyumbani managed to persuade Justine to organise the court hearing for Friday. This is a weight off our minds. Writser went with Dick this afternoon to the Spirit of Faith (our host's orphanage), the children had an hour's sleep for once and I had some peace and quiet. It did me the world of good!

This evening Maggie and I plaited Mette's hair Kenyan style. She sat still for one and a half hours while Writser distracted her. We want her to look good for the court case. Writser and I are in much higher spirits today. By the way, Mette's hair (which she calls 'rope') looks wonderful and it was only done by two amateurs. She says that she looks like a clown, and it's true. Bye…till the next e-mail.

28 March, 19.12 hours
Thanks for your e-mails. Today it didn't rain, which was nice. Mette wasn't too well yesterday evening, her new hair was hurting her. For the first time in her life we gave her a children's paracetamol. She then fell asleep in my arms. Wisse goes about his business and laughs, says 'dadadada, mama-mama' and that's about all. But we understand him well because he points to things clearly. He has a massive appetite, just like Mette, and now finishes off what Mette leaves. Tomorrow she can have the pot of baby food we brought for Wisse. Wisse just eats what the rest of us eat…

Tomorrow we're going to the embassy to get the papers for the *laissez-passer* (ever the optimists) and while we're there we'll ask which four documents we need again, as we don't want to find out something's missing at the last moment. We've been through all that before so we'll do anything to avoid the same thing happening again. And by then it'll be nearly Friday!

29 March 19.09 hours
Today was another day filled with surprises. It was a particularly good day today considering how caught up we are mentally preparing ourselves for tomorrow. Today we had to go to the embassy, just to be on the safe side, for the papers we will be needing. For Mette there were four different documents, but after the trouble we had last week we want to be absolutely sure about the type of documents so that we won't be taken by surprise

again. First, we had to wait of course, but as they remember us from last time, we were up quite soon. We already had passport size photos of Wisse and the man from the embassy gave us the papers. He said that it is all we'll need and asked us at what time we wanted to pick up the *laissez-passer*. We asked him to confirm which papers are needed, but he had received a letter from the Netherlands saying that he could issue a *laissez-passer* without the need for any additional papers. That means that as soon as the judge finalises the adoption tomorrow, which we're sure he will do, we can pick up the adoption order in the afternoon. And that means we can come back to the Netherlands! (It's true that other papers still need to be organised, but if the embassy doesn't need them now then it can wait for a later KLM trip or we'll send them by courier). We don't understand the logic behind it all but choose to just accept it. Tomorrow at the end of the morning we can pick up the provisional passport!!!

We've arranged to stay with Dick and Maggie a little longer. We've been very stressed up to now and it shows. We're going to wait for the weekend before booking our stand-by seats with KLM. We'll check that situation out tomorrow, too. If all goes as hoped, we'll have a good-bye party in Nyumbani, probably on Monday. We celebrated all this good news and our high expectations with a cup of coffee. And a cream slice for Writser, of course!

We love having Wisse around. Mette is still not quite herself. Tonight, she ate almost all of Wisse's pot of baby food. It's obvious she's lost weight. We really feel for her, but there's not much we can do apart from go along with it until she's back to normal. Wisse's covered in fleabites, but that can be expected in a house full of so many dirty dogs? I disinfected his entire cot today and he's wearing new pyjamas.

We're off to the lawyer's early tomorrow. The court opens at nine o'clock and then it's a question of awaiting our turn. Maybe we'll know more before you've got up, with only two hours' time difference. We'll e-mail as soon as we have some news, but we have some things to attend to in the city, so we don't know exactly when we'll be back. We're optimistic, especially after today...

30 March, 15.58 hours
Dear all: we got it! It was one hell of a day today, Writser sighed: will the stress never end? But the stress is now over and now it´s your turn, because if KLM will take us, and it looks like they will, we'll be coming home on 1 April. NOT JOKING!!! This means we'll be landing at 6:10 and we'll be through customs at about half past six. A nice and early Sunday morning for whoever is picking us up!

Some things went really quickly, such as getting Wisse's provisional passport, and then this morning there was a big hassle again in court. First of all, our awful lawyer wasn't there, but luckily there was someone to replace her. We didn't know her but she was very well informed and most involved. Nicolas, the social worker, wasn't there, and neither was the woman from the Kenyan Child Protection Agency. And in this country the case is not allowed to proceed without them. The judge of course immediately asked where everyone was. It turned out that they had been sitting outside the court room, because they hadn't expected us to be the first in court at nine o'clock. Typical Kenyan mentality, they were sitting on the bench in the corridor because they didn't dare to just walk in (Kenyan reserve). We were close to wetting ourselves with nerves, because the judge could easily have postponed the case and then the place would have been shut down until after the Easter holidays. But miracles do happen! And after a long period of silence and tension, the judge let us go with the comment that it wasn't in accordance with her rules, but that she would let us go *with* the children. The new lawyer certainly made her contribution by pointing out to the judge that it was only a matter of presenting a follow-up programme and that we could now do that. Maybe it wouldn't have worked out if Justine had been handling our case still...

We both shed lots of tears and even now as I write I have a lump in my throat. We could hardly believe it. At the lawyer's office we phoned home quickly with the request that everyone else on the phone list should be called and told the news. What an indescribably wonderful feeling!

This afternoon, we picked up our adoption order, i.e. the original document confirming the judge's granting of the adoption. Yesterday, a small miracle, we already had permission to pick up Wisse's *laissez-passer* from the embassy without needing any additional papers (for Mette we needed four different papers and another two weeks of waiting) and we'd sorted that out, too, by the end of the afternoon. When we went to check with KLM to see how the booking figures were coming along for the following week, things did not look too good. Our best chances for getting seats were on Saturday evening, so we booked them without delay. It's a real pity that there won't be a good-bye party at Nyumbani, but we'll certainly be back again another time. Plus our children have had more than enough. Wisse has developed quite a bad cough and you've all read plenty about Mette's stress. So assuming there are no more setbacks, we'll be back home Sunday morning. After all this tension we never dared to dream that this would happen. In fact, we still can't really believe it, and we're walking round in a bit of a daze. It's almost as if we're thinking: what could still go wrong? But actually nothing else *can* go wrong, and in a minute I'm going to go and see what to pack and what to leave behind. Tomorrow afternoon, we're going to the hotel because it's easier to get to the airport from there. We'll also meet the KLM crew we'll be flying back with. Alright, enough for now, we're going to open a bottle of champagne with Dick and Maggie and just sit back and relax. Thank you for all your moral support all your e-mails. We wouldn't have survived without them, because we both found this whole experience totally draining and support from the home front is the only thing that cheered us up a bit (apart from the wonderful support from Dick and Maggie). Lots of love from Writser, Geeri, Mette AND WISSE!

We sent a special e-mail to my sister later that day. It was her birthday and we were delighted to give her the most wonderful gift she could have wished for: a nephew!

31 March - 1 April

Mette recognised the hotel, realised that the dogs were gone and regained her liveliness. It was a bizarre thing to witness. We had the cot put in our room again and had a wonderful day. It also turned out that the purser and his wife (both on duty on the flight for that evening) were acquaintances of ours and this, combined with the favourable booking figures, made us confident that we would be able to travel home that evening. We had no idea of the disappointment ahead of us.

Well on time, we went to the airport with all our luggage and headed straight for the check-in desk. The procedure is to wait there until you are called up, then you get a seat number and may board the aircraft. This always involves waiting until the very last moment. So we were not at all worried as the crew walked off through customs with a "see you later" wave and a broad smile. We sat waiting patiently on our chairs. It was only as the take-off time came uncomfortably close that we went to the ground crew, whom we also knew well by now, to enquire about the situation. It turned out that there were no more available seats. For unknown reasons the plane had filled up completely and we would not be able to leave until the next morning on a Kenya Airways flight. We had to find somewhere to spend the night, as we had already checked out of the hotel. We could not believe our ears. I must have asked them to check about four times and then started to panic. We had been so sure of getting seats on this plane. All of us were completely exhausted and I could barely think straight. However unbelievable, it was true. At least we were able to leave our luggage at the airport until the following morning, so all we needed to do was put the two sleeping children into a taxi and return to the hotel in the hopes that there would be a room available for us. We asked the ground crew staff to call the hotel for us and inform them of our situation, but other than that there was nothing more they could do to help. Mette woke up when we entered the hotel again and almost freaked out. Wisse also woke up and thought it was all a great adventure. We then had to sort everything out for the night. As our own travel cot was now at the airport, we needed two cots for the night and that took forever to arrange. We also had to phone the Netherlands without delay so that those picking us up would know not to come that morning. We would instead be arriving early in the evening. One phone call to my brother set the communication apparatus in full flow. There we sat on the big bed with two children who did not want to sleep – Mette was crying, Wisse was fascinated with what was going on around him. And as for us, all we wanted was peace and quiet to get over yet another disappointment. We were so totally fed up, I can still picture us sitting on that bed…

The next morning, we were up at the crack of dawn, had breakfast quickly and went straight to the airport. There, we were given a warm welcome and were allocated seat numbers immediately. We then passed through customs as quickly as possible, just to get it over with, as you never know what new setbacks might be in store. But fortunately nothing went wrong at all. We went upstairs and sat down, let the children run around, looked at the two buggies and kept our thoughts to ourselves. Whenever I am in Nairobi airport and see those seats, I think of how we felt at that moment: utterly exhausted, prepared for new setbacks and looking forward to going home, hoping that it would put an end to our misery.

The journey was wonderful. The children were in great spirits, although two young children are a handful, but still we enjoyed every minute. We were on our way home!! At last! Unbelievable! After eight and a half hours we reached the Netherlands and hastily disembarked. The colleague who had been waiting for us at the gate with balloons when we arrived with Mette was there again to greet us. We passed through customs to discover that we were missing a suitcase. That did not concern us too much, but reporting it took at least three quarters of an hour. Three quarters of an hour while our relatives in the arrival hall were hermetically sealed off from us, and our colleague being the only one able to communicate between the two sides. We had decided that we would walk out into the arrival hall together as a family and not just one of us with the children. So there was still more waiting, but this time, our relatives felt it most.

Everything worked out fine in the end. We had tea with traditional Dutch biscuits and were given cake in the crew centre where everyone admired Wisse. We still experienced a lot of inner confusion, there were plenty of tears of relief and sheer exhaustion. We were relieved and proud. Mette showed Wisse the crew centre. After all, she had been there often and enjoyed her role as the big sister. Wisse loved the whole adventure and ran around the big room. We were not only congratulated by our relatives and friends but also by many colleagues who were at Schiphol to begin their day's work. Many knew of our undertaking and could now see its direct result running about. After we had let everyone see our latest miracle, we only wanted one thing: to go home. Writser fetched the car, Mette sat in her own seat and Wisse sat on my lap. If felt unusual to be driving home as a complete family. And this was what it would be like from now on: husband, wife, two children. Incredible.

Once again, we were roused from our daze by the sight of a brightly decorated street with many of our neighbours standing waiting for us impatiently, coffees in hands. It was now much later than expected, what with the extra delay of the lost suitcase. But the sincerity of the welcome was overwhelming. The welcome my mother gave us moved us to tears. The neighbours had been spoiling her while she waited for the moment when she could at last admire her granddaughter and grandson. Mette clung to her tightly, convinced that no harm could come to her as long as she had her grandmother with her. My mother had missed Mette terribly and could see by her thin face that it had been a hard time for her.

That evening, we let Mette run all around the house while we lay Wisse in his cot. For some time now, Mette had been sleeping in a child's bed and she agreed that the cot was now the place for her little brother to sleep, next to mummy and daddy's big bed. I need not tell that we all fell into bed early that evening feeling exhausted, but so very happy.

In the middle of the night, I heard Writser get out of bed. He was not feeling well and my nurse's instinct made me feel his forehead. It was burning up, which was no good sign. I put two and two together: two weeks in Kenya, 10 days' incubation time: malaria. So we used the night not to sleep, but to make a plan for the following day. Writser would go to the doctor at a quarter past eight who would give him a referral. I would stay at home with the children. Writser would have to take a taxi to the hospital for a thick-blood film test for malaria. The night eventually passed, and in the end it turned out to be 'only' bronchitis with a high fever, which at least was not as bad as malaria. But I will never forget that first day: Writser really ill, Wisse coughing and sniffling and Mette exhausted yet hyperactive because she was back home again. I actually should have been out getting practical things such as a high-chair, a children's car seat, food, drink, clothes for Wisse, arrival cards, stamps, etc. As we had not dared to buy these things in advance, we were now badly equipped. From time to time, thanks to the balloons and streamers, we had lots of beloved well-wishers coming in to congratulate us and bring us flowers. I still feel uneasy looking back on that day. Luckily, I have a hardy husband who, despite a high fever, accompanied me on fetching the majority of the heavy objects. At last we had all necessities in stock. The arrival had been a success and our family was now complete.

Four weeks later, we threw an arrival party. It was wonderful, we had a traditional barrel organ and an ice-cream van. Wisse behaved as if he had been living in the Netherlands for years and welcomed all the attention as he played with the other children.

After Wisse's arrival in the Netherlands, it was now Writser who would stay home with the children while I went out to earn us a living. It felt so strange, having just had another child yet getting straight back into the routine of things. It was hard for me at first. We would not have our first holiday until August, which was still a long way off. But I managed to get back to the old everyday life, which gradually became easier.

In the meantime, the procedure for registering with the aliens police had undergone several changes and was now wholly by correspondence. We did go to register Wisse with the town hall registrar and paid a visit to the doctor's, and Wisse had his first visit to the consultation office to see the children's nurse. He turned out to be in excellent health, only suffering from a bit of a rash, a cough and a cold, but nothing serious. At the aliens police, things were bureaucratic and slow, and the papers we had received were skimmed through and mostly put aside. We applied for guardianship under Dutch law with the help from our friend the lawyer and everything seemed settled. Wisse adapted effortlessly and we wrote our report every three months like good students, and sent it to the Child Protection Agency in Africa and also sent a copy to the Africa Foundation in the Netherlands. We thought we had everything well under control. In August we went to our regular campsite in France with a big tent and let all the campers we had met the year before admire our family addition. Writser had worked at the site as a student and was therefore more than a guest. Everyone had been deeply sympathetic and could now see the fruit of our labours. It was a busy time, busier than we had expected and the big bag full of books we had taken with us went back home practically untouched, but we had had a wonderful holiday!

On a sadder note, there were a number of deaths in my family. After my father, who had died so suddenly after Mette's arrival, his older brother died equally suddenly six months later. An uncle passed away that year, followed by another one at the end of the year. The year 2002 began with another bereavement, a very dear friend of ours lost his father. We had been together for New Year's Eve at our friends' house, and his father had been there too. Very suddenly and unexpectedly, his life came to an end. We were all shaken. I heard the awful news when I returned from Los Angeles with a pack of life savers (he was very into American jokes) that I had brought back for father Piet. Two weeks later, we were back in church for yet another funeral, this time of a dear aunt of mine whom I had visited often as a child. As well as my own sadness, there was the sadness of my cousins who had now lost their mother after having lost their father the previous year. There seemed to be no end to reducing the numbers of our family. So much grief in such a short period of time.

Our next holiday was due in March, and we were very much looking forward to going skiing for two weeks and having a complete change of scenery to recover from all the emotions. But this holiday also turned out to be quite different than we had hoped. Mette fell ill on the first day. Wisse followed suit on Friday and was in a particularly sorry state, full of mucus and a very nasty cough. Mette seemed to slowly be getting better, so I took her with me into the village to buy a thermometer. We had not needed one before. Wisse's temperature was 38.5 and when we took Mette's because she thought it looked interesting, it showed she had a temperature of over 39. So we all set off to the doctor's. Both children were diagnosed with an ear infection and Wisse also had bronchitis. It was not hard to believe, quite heart-breaking to listen to. Writser would go skiing on Sunday and I was going to take a skiing lesson on Monday morning, so that we could take turns in making the best of a splendid Austrian winter (for we were having world-class weather).

On Sunday morning, I did not feel one hundred percent; so I took my temperature and saw that I had a fever, as well. I did not want to tell Writser until he was back from the ski slopes, and actually did not feel that bad. To be on the safe side, I went to see the doctor, because I rarely got a fever and we still had a week's holiday ahead us. I was diagnosed with a double ear infection – so much for the skiing! And yet my ears did not particularly hurt. In the afternoon, we went for a drive in the car, but after the very first hill I had had enough. When my ears popped, it was all over for me. Meanwhile, the children had stopped eating and drinking. Mette could not hold anything down, which was very unlike her, and Wisse simply would not swallow anything. We were both worried about the high fever, though it seemed to have improved by Monday morning. Mette ate vanilla pudding and Wisse had two mouthfuls. Writser was going to take my skiing lesson and I would somehow manage to look after the two children. I took a couple of aspirins against the fever and as long as I kept my head straight, it was bearable. But as soon as Writser was packing his skiing equipment, Mette was sick again. The bedroom was one big mess, then suddenly we noticed that Wisse was covered in diarrhoea. I burst into tears. All I wanted was to go home. My apparently strong character could not take any more. There was no longer any point putting on a brave face and thinking I could manage everything – I could not. I had reached the very end of my tether. Bin bags were hastily filled with dirty clothes covered in sick and whatnot and we threw everything into the car, informed the apartment's owner (who was at her job) that we were going home and at midday, drove off, in tears and a very bad mood. We drove full steam ahead back to the Netherlands, our two sick children in the back seat. The children were in a daze throughout the journey, refusing to eat or drink anything, and Wisse's eyes were turning skywards. It was an absolute drama. We stopped at the hospital near our house where we were admitted without a referral or phone call from our GP, for Wisse's condition seemed quite serious. Eventually, we managed a sigh of relief. The Austrian doctor's diagnosis was confirmed, but despite the dehydration symptoms they considered it safe to let us all go home. By midnight, we had made it to our own beds. Our holiday was over.

From April to October 2002

I stayed at home until mid-April. 1 April, "Wisse day", we commemorated with a Chinese dinner. My first flight after my sick leave was to Mexico. When I returned from that, Writser told me he had some bad news. I thought we might be in for more tolling funeral bells, but it was something else, he said. Something worse.

Two days before I arrived back at Schiphol, I was away on duty, we had received a letter from the IND (Immigration and Naturalisation Department) saying that Wisse was going to be deported.

One of the last sentences of the letter was: "Please inform us by what means you plan to leave the country."

My first reaction was to laugh it off, scoffing that it was not likely to come to that, but it did not take long for reality to hit. Writser had of course already contacted the lawyer who had tackled our problems during the adoption procedures, who confirmed that this was indeed no joke. It was quite serious. Stress was back with a vengeance. In short: we started to think up emergency strategies, escape plans, plans to go and live in Kenya or go underground, etc. We wasted no time and went back to Kenya several times in the quest for the papers that the IND wanted to see, but we did not have and would never get our hands on if the Kenyan lawyer and Kenyan authorities had their way. According to the IND in the Netherlands, a stamp was missing, yet in Kenya we were told that putting the stamp on the papers rendered them invalid under Kenyan law. Nobody understood the logic of this. We sat sweating it out in the offices of various Kenyan authorities. We were dealing with forms we had never heard of and certainly had not needed for Mette's adoption. We saw offices we had never seen before and met people we had never needed before. Our Dutch lawyer did not permit us to directly contact the IND. He now acted as intermediary to prevent us from making any possibly fatal mistakes. We were fine with this, as we were at a complete loss. Our child, our Wisse, whom we had fought so hard for, was to go back to Kenya? A ludicrous idea, but however impossible it seemed to us, our lawyer (a down to earth and supportive man, who also happened to have a good sense of humour) assured us it was in fact a very realistic possibility.

With the help of friendly officials and the embassy staff in Kenya, we finally found the stamps we thought we needed. Thought, because we were never entirely sure what was required. It was yet another period to send our stress levels sky high. The timing alone was enough to do that. Emotionally and physically, we were just finding our feet again and had only just regained some energy to face the outside world again. All of a sudden, the accumulated emotions of the last years came flooding back. And this was their breaking point. There was no more putting on a brave face for family and friends. This letter and the threatening consequences completely numbed us. After the intense struggle we had been through to adopt our second child, there was suddenly another battle to be fought. We were not prepared for it and we certainly had not built up the resilience it would demand of us.

Meanwhile, from 1 April the procedure was being hurried along to approve the adoption under Dutch law, and at the end of December, we were informed that the judge had finalised the procedure. Wisse was to be granted Dutch nationality. We knew that it would take another three months before this procedure would be concluded, but there we stood, holding the letter with tears in our eyes. Mette stood by and asked cautiously: "Are those happy tears?" Although she could not understand the details of it, she had instinctively felt that something was wrong. I remember returning from Kenya one time with a pile of important, stamped papers for Wisse's adoption case. We went out for a Chinese meal to celebrate and asked Mette if she had any idea why we were doing that (we only went to the Chinese restaurant on Mette-day or Wisse-day). She immediately replied: "Yes, because Wisse can stay." Honestly!

Two thousand and two, a tearful year with no end of troubles. And that is without mentioning our catastrophic summer holiday in France, when on 9 September we lost our tent and all its contents in the floods in the de Gard region. We drove home in an empty car feeling destitute as soon as the roads were reopened. I was tired throughout the year, could not cope with anything, suffered frequent headaches and colds, underwent acupuncture and shiatsu treatment, had saunas – all to no avail. In physical terms, it was a disastrous year. But finally, the much longed-for document arrived at the end of December. On 2 April 2003, Wisse was included in our passports and we felt safe.

Our lawyer advised us, however, not to contact the IND, for he had heard of some very troublesome cases.

Recap

Reading back what I have written, I realise that I have spoken only little of our children. Perhaps this is a pity for the reader, for they are wonderful children and a continuous source of joy to us. Children who warm you, children worth fighting for – and what children are not? Children who, I realise while writing this, were worth the crying and praying.

But this book is not primarily about children. There are plenty of books about children. This book is about the pitfalls and perils, the twists and turns along the road to adoption. It is a unique journey, but other people's adoption stories will have much in common with your own. They are all bumpy, obstacle-strewn roads.

Being better prepared for obstacles means less surprises and more enjoyment both before and afterwards.

If you are better prepared, you will be better equipped in two ways. You will be better equipped in terms of tools to get you through the difficult times and better equipped physically for the arrival of the child.

Knowing what to expect certainly should not make you doubt about adopting a child. Books that tell pregnant women about the possibilities of tiredness, nausea, heartburn, pelvic instability, painful and swollen breasts, itching, stretch marks, painful birth, etc. are a given in the world today. Their warnings have not kept couples from having children.

This book aims to give prospective adoptive parents a chance to prepare themselves for a special time in their lives. I feel this should also be a given in the world.

Our story is an example. We did not take enough time to savour the moments that were worth savouring. We did not take any breaks though we could have. The second part of this book offers suggestions for dealing with things differently. We may well have experienced less stress if I had trained as a stress consultant beforehand instead of after. But perhaps then I would not have chosen this subject and therefore not benefited from my training, either. The training has taught me to see events that cause stress in a different way. Let me say that I hope you will succeed at this, too.

I wish you good luck and enjoyment with the adoption of your child.

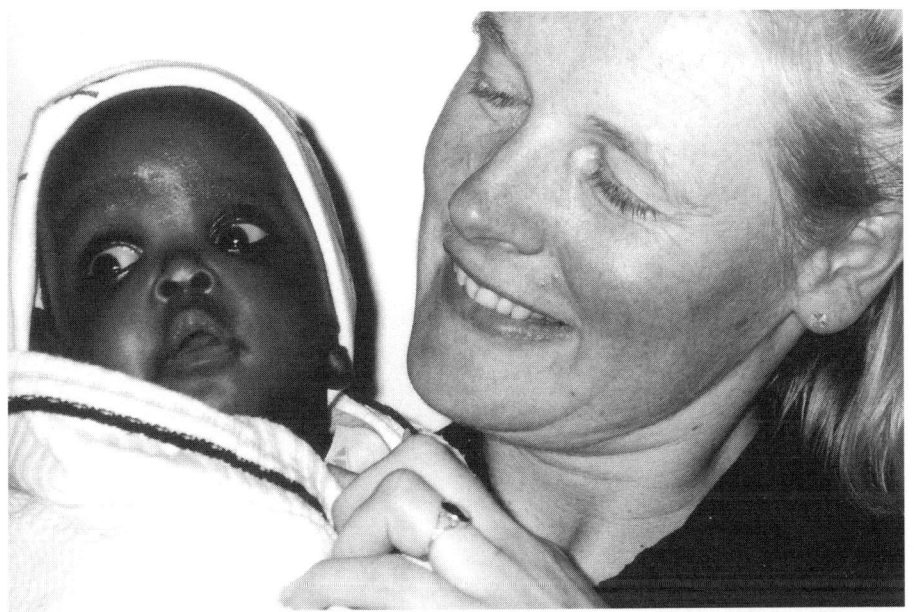

22 april 1999, the first encounter with Mette, at that time still called Salomé.

2 may 1999, the baptism of Mette Joanne Salomé.

2 may 1999, after the baptism, gathering of the new family.

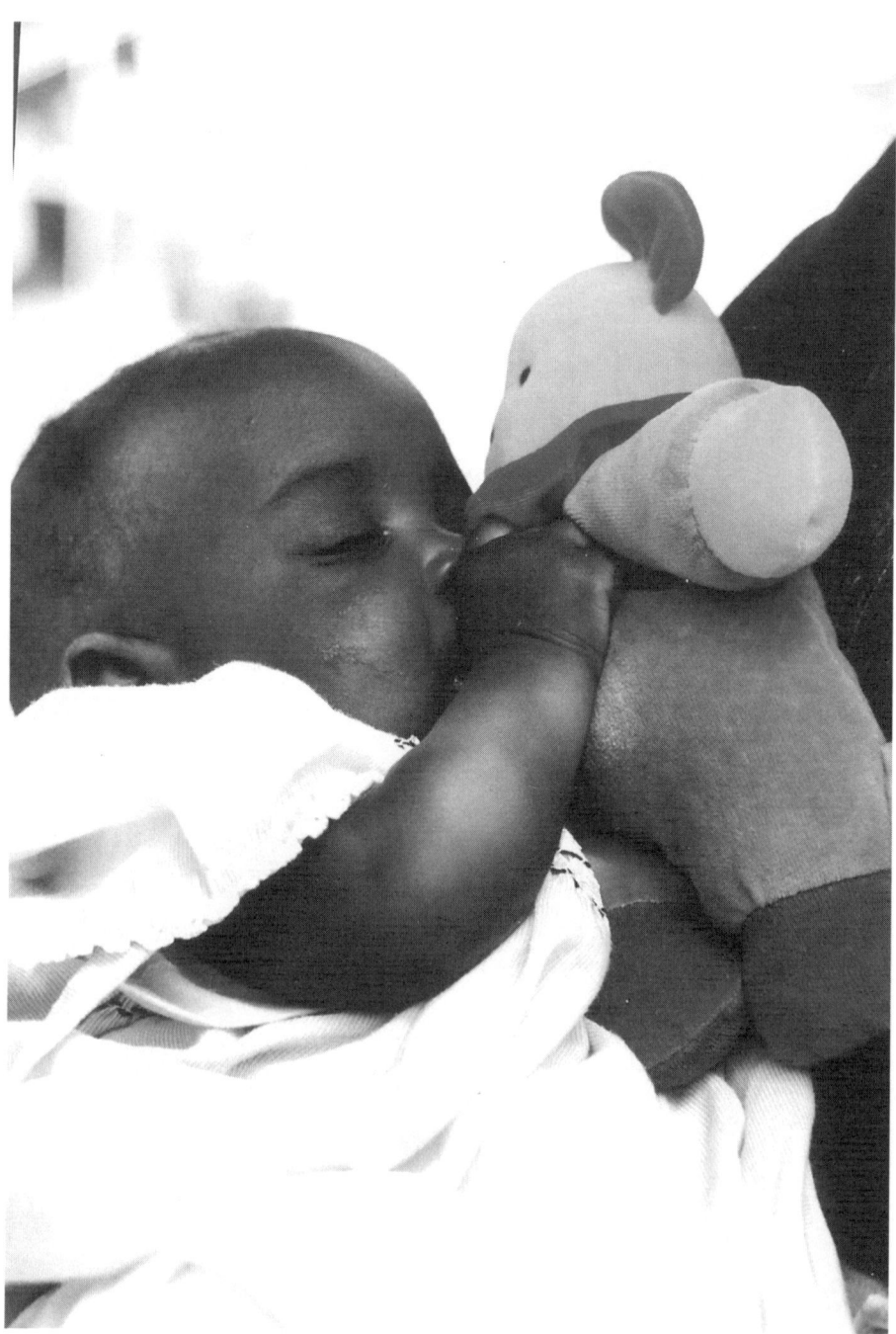
Mette's little doll.

26 october 1999. The day of the courtcase, waiting.

Eating our special biscuits after the approval of the judge.

We used this picture for Mette's arrival card.

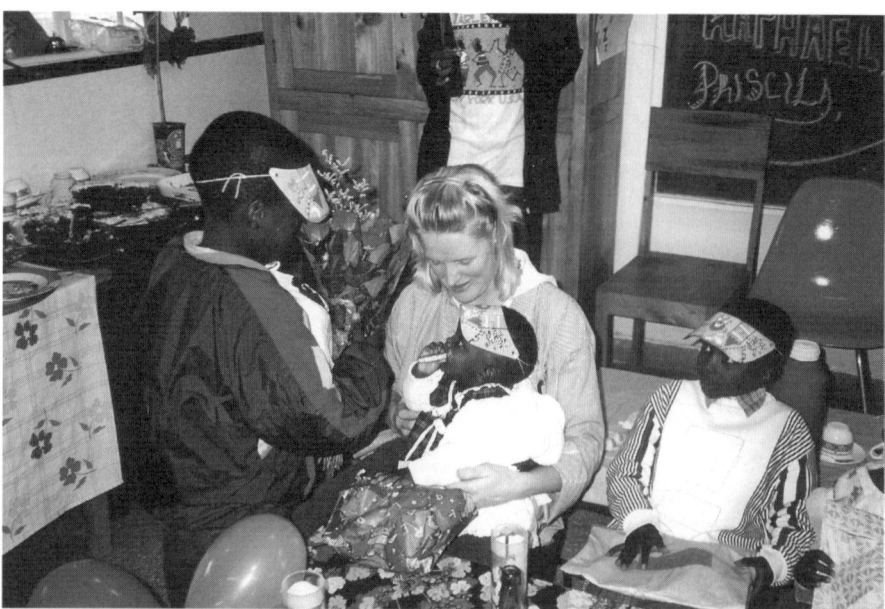
Mette's first birthday.

Waving goodbye with mama Elisabeth.

Going home with mom, dad and Mette.

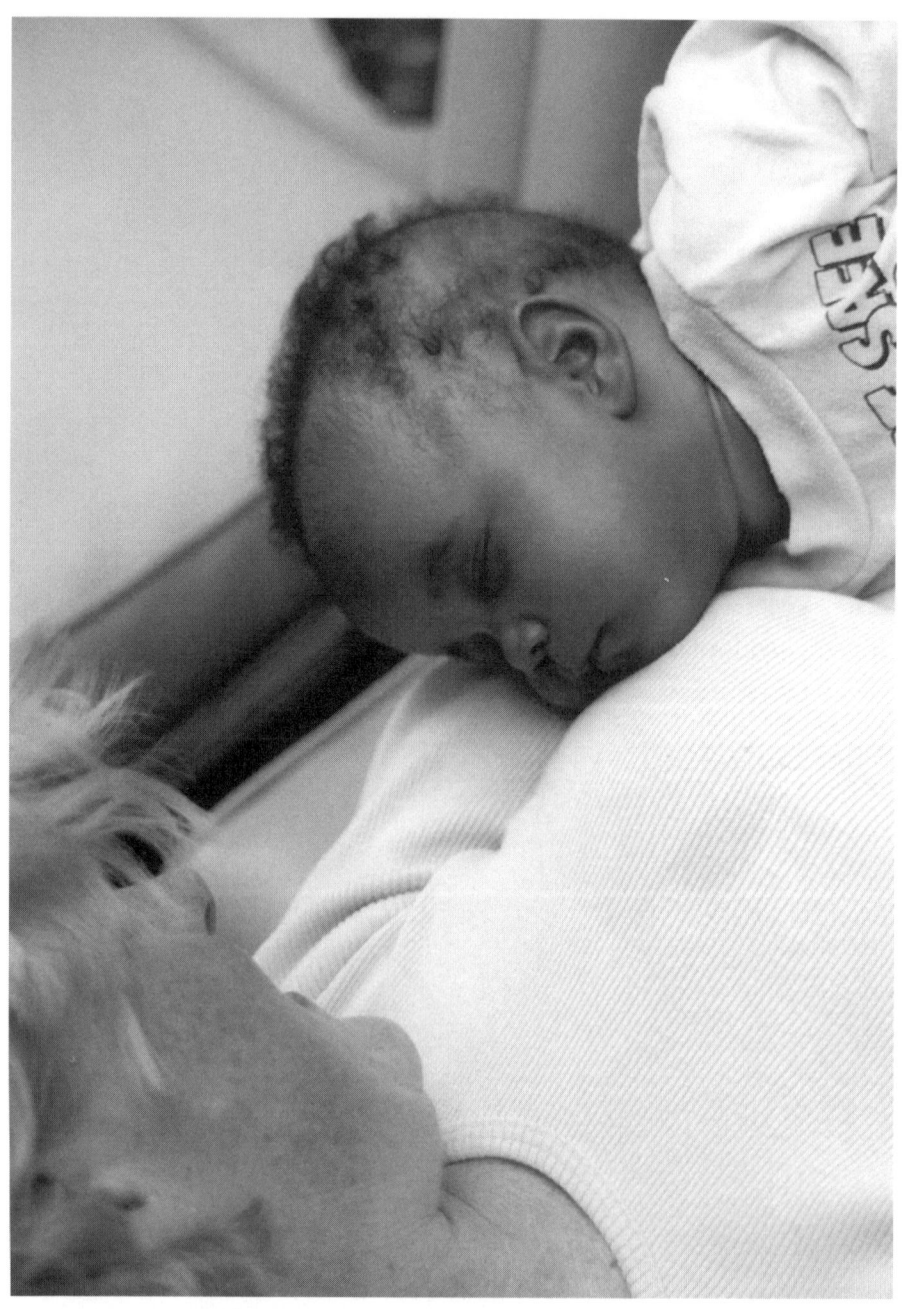

11 april 2000, the first encounter with Wisse, at that time still called Steven.

Together with me.

Already driving his car.

Together with dad.

Together with mama Beatrice.

Celebrating Wisse's birthday.

Just after his birthday, his first steps in Nyumbani.

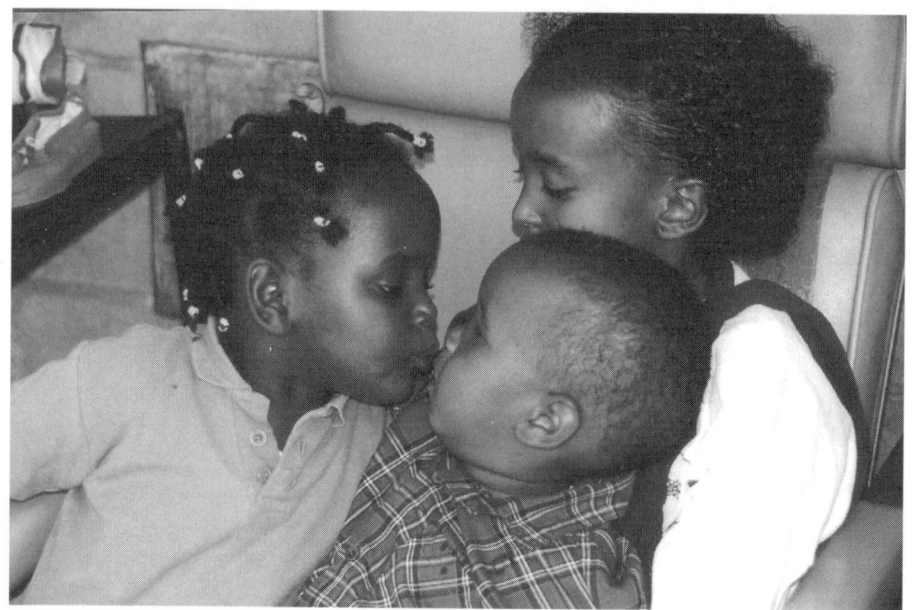

22 march 2001, Mette's first kiss to Wisse.

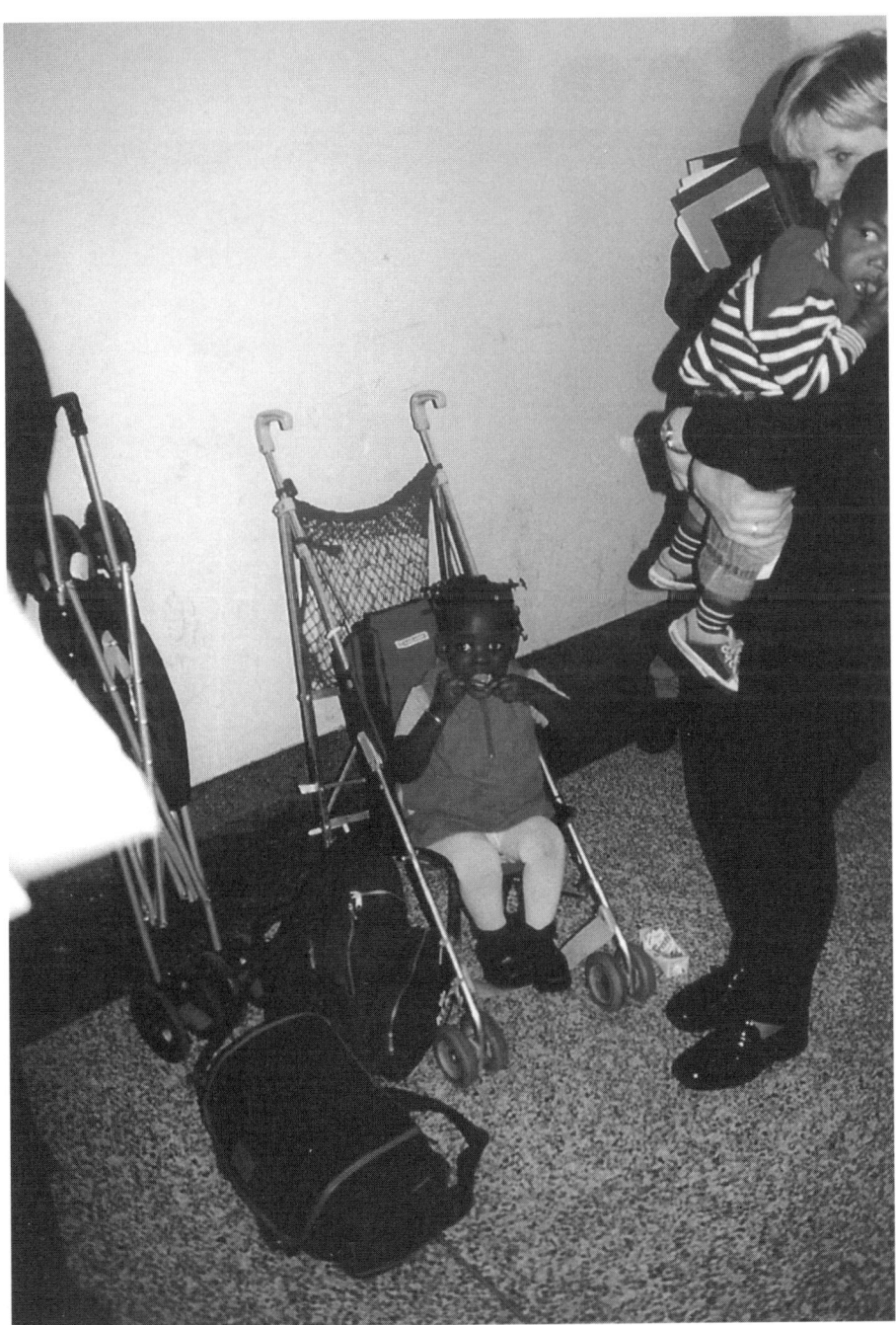

Waiting at the court to enter the courtroom.

Going home with mom and dad.

2
Step by step

The survey

I found many candidates keen to participate in the survey I conducted on stress during the period of the adoption procedure. I came to read other adoption stories, and each story was as intense as the next, and all were worthy of being made into a book.

This is a summary of some of the results of a survey that I carried out among a group of adoptive parents.

- Almost every adoption experiences moments of stress (unhealthy tension).
- Men and women experience the same events differently.
- During the entire adoption procedure, feelings of stress are not dealt with.
- Feelings of stress are not necessarily related to the seriousness of the situation at a particular moment.
- Feelings of powerlessness and anger are regular occurrences.
- People who are dependent on an adoption agency experience the wait as highly frustrating.
- It is crucial to be able to discuss everything with your partner for the whole process to be a success.
- Despite the cost (some people have to save up in order to be able to adopt), financial consequences transpire as being quite a small stress factor.

- Men often find the adoption procedure less stressful than the hospital visits that often precede it, because they no longer have to look on helplessly while women undergo unpleasant experiments and treatment.
- The hospital visits preceding many adoptions are often still fresh in the adoptive parents' minds, or in some cases still continue.
- Taking steps together with other couples (for example, going as a group to pick up a child from China) helps to reduce feelings of stress or deal with them more effectively.
- Adoptions concluded via an adoption agency and adoptions achieved by independent adoptive parents are subject to different moments of stress.
- Independent adoptive parents tend to experience more stress in the country where the adoption is taking place, while the other group experiences more stress in the Netherlands as they wait for news from the adoption agency.
- Women usually experience more stress than men during the adoption procedure.
- Adoptive parents complain of insomnia, fatigue, neck pains, headaches, stomach aches, weight loss, allergies, exacerbation of existing psychosomatic problems, depression, emotional problems and in some cases even psychosis.

Equipped with this information, I took on the challenge of this new adventure: writing this book. Step by step, working towards the ultimate goal: a child of your own to love.

The procedure

The decision to adopt is normally taken after a period in which couples have tried to get pregnant. Studies show that some ninety per cent of couples opting for adoption first tried natural pregnancy. The authorities in the Netherlands advise couples to first come to terms with this period before embarking on the process of adoption. In practice, the couples' intense desire to have a child usually results in them applying for adoption while the medical procedures are just winding down or in some cases are still in full swing. After all, the 2006 statistics show that at least three and a half years pass from the moment of application for adoption until the arrival of the adoptive child. The second group of people wanting to adopt are those who have idealistic motives for choosing adoption. They often already have one or more children of their own and wish to extend their family with an adoptive child. There is also a group of people who choose for single-parent adoption. The procedure described below is based on the situation in the Netherlands. Procedures in other countries may vary.

Registering with the Dutch Foundation for Adoption Services, is a question of paperwork, writing letters or phoning them. They send you the application form and you and your partner fill it in together. Then the wait begins.

Waiting for news that the procedure can actually begin takes about 22 months, based on the situation in 2006. A few months after registering, you are requested to transfer approximately 900 euros (six years ago it was about half that sum) and you are put on the list to participate in a compulsory VIA information course of six afternoons. More waiting.

Candidates often quite enjoy *waiting for the course,* although now the waiting period is much longer than it used to be. But the knowledge that something is happening is comforting.

Participation in the so-called VIA courses is compulsory for all prospective adoptive parents to participate. The course is named after the organisation that organises it, the Centre for Information on the Adoption of Foreign Children. Employers must grant time off work to attend this course. This is often the moment the employer is told about adoption plans, and you find yourself compelled to come out of anonymity. Issues handled during the course include your motive for adopting, the choice of a particular country, the procedures, bonding with the child, and the problems often encountered with adoptive children. The composition of the group in which you are placed largely determines the extent to which you will enjoy the course. In our case, for example, we are still in touch with some of the couples from our VIA course group, but not all groups produce lasting acquaintances.

Waiting for meetings with the Child Protection Agency are a given. They are to be expected as a part of the whole procedure and most people accept this without too much trouble. This is not to say that the meetings are found to be very enjoyable. As a particularly motivated prospective parent, your suitability for parenthood is assessed while the majority of parents in the country get pregnant and have children with no questions asked. The degree of stress these sessions cause largely depends on the person assessing your suitability as a parent. Depending on the region, there are between two and five sessions, at least one of which takes place at your home.

The "consent in principle", stating that you are suitable to go ahead with the adoption procedure, is awarded after completion of the VIA course and the meetings with the Child Protection Agency. It comes in the form of a report. Only a very small percentage of cases are refused the consent principle. You are allowed to read the consent principle, but you may not keep it. It is eventually sent to the adoption agency of your choice.

It is at this stage that the procedure may continue in two different ways. On the one hand, there is the group of people who hire the services of a licensed, i.e. adoption, agency, in order to proceed with the adoption. On the other hand, there is a group of people who already have, or plan to obtain, a contact address abroad from which they wish to organise the adoption themselves. People in this group are known as 'independent' adoptive parents.

Each group experiences different periods and moments of stress. I will therefore deal with the procedure for each group separately, beginning with the people who organise their adoption through an adoption agency.

The adoption agency procedure

Registering with the adoption agency is of course the first step. The choice of agency is often determined by the choice of a particular country, for not all agencies are active in all countries of the world. You will come across terms such as "contract countries" and "non-contract countries" (or similar), depending on whether your country has concluded a legalised adoption contract with that country. Adoption agencies can only organise adoptions from so-called contract countries.

At the moment of registering with an agency, the prospective parents may be opting for a child from China (and therefore often a girl), or a child from South Africa (which sometimes involves living in that country for several months), et cetera. Opting for a particular country means committing yourself and simultaneously choosing not to adopt a child from another country, because you can only have one procedure running at a time.

From this point onwards, it may take between one and four years before the child arrives in your family.

The meeting or meetings with the adoption agency. You may have to cope with extremely intimate questions. One of the many difficult questions you will be asked is whether you are prepared to adopt a child with a handicap. The answers you give have far-reaching implications.

Waiting for news from the adoption agency certainly marks one of the most difficult periods in the procedure, and can sometimes take years. Even a pregnant elephant does not have to wait this long for its baby!

Some parents already start *decorating the baby's room*. This may pose a problem, as you do not know if you will eventually adopt a baby, a toddler or a slightly older child.

After the wait, the agency eventually *allocates a child to you* and you receive a photo of the child. Once this has happened, the journey to pick up the child (or its arrival at the airport) usually happens quite quickly. What now needs to be attended to is the *preparation for the journey*, i.e. vaccinations, travel documents, etc. This is generally a very hectic but wonderful time, because soon it will all be over. However, in some cases changed circumstances in the child's country of origin can deliver some unpleasant surprises. In 2003, for example, the outbreak of SARS caused long delays for adoptions from China.

The journey is generally organised and coordinated entirely by the adoption agency. Most adoptive parents-to-be prefer this. Generally, a group of couples will travel together to pick up their future children, and they experience such joint journeys as a great source of support. The child or children are normally placed with the future parents after one or two days. This is followed by an emotional period of getting used to each other, when expectations become a reality. There may also be disappointment.

After the journey, it is time to *travel back home*. It is inevitably a very emotional time when the child is integrated in the family home, which from then on will never be the same.

The initial period at home is particularly special. The VIA course strongly advises plenty of rest in the beginning, so that child and parents have time to grow accustomed to each other and the bonding process has the best chance of succeeding. As well as resting well, there is the pile of paperwork to attend to. The child must be registered in the municipality of residence or, in the case of an adoption from a non-contract country, with the aliens police. Soon after returning home, you also have to take your child to the doctor's, the consultation office and the hospital.

Then what is left is the *financial bloodletting and the final paperwork*. In the Netherlands, the adoption procedure under Dutch law by which a child is given Dutch nationality, can start only after a child has been in the country for a year. Adoptive parents tend to say little about the financial aspects. The situation is such, that for financially less well-off members of Dutch society, the ability to adopt even one child, let alone several children, cannot be taken for granted.

The approximate costs in the Netherlands in 2006 were as follows:

€ 900 for the VIA information course;
€ 7,500 to € 22,700 in mediation fees for the agency;
€ 600 for finalising the adoption under Dutch law (one year after arrival).

(Source: Ministry of Justice, www.adoptie.nl)

The independent adoptive parents procedure

Independent adoptive parents will experience different moments of stress, related to the different actions they have to take. First they must *seek and establish contact abroad.* Personal motives often make people choose to adopt from a particular country, perhaps because they have lived there, have friends or family there, or have already met a child there. In most cases, the choice is a clear and justifiable one and the prospective parents do not have or wish for any alternative.

Independent adoptive parents also have to find an adoption agency to act as partial mediator. The contact address, which they have provided themselves, must be screened for reliability in order to prevent child trafficking. Not all adoption agencies are happy about independent adopters. In many cases a meeting is held with the adoption agency in question before the partial mediation can begin.

In the country of adoption, the DIY adopters have to organise everything themselves. This ranges from finding a reliable lawyer to, in most cases, having to attend court proceedings in that particular country. *All necessary transactions, all forms of contact with the authorities and all court fees* must be financed by the independent adopter. An unexpected turn of events may occur at any time. Prospective parents are confronted with a different culture, a different way of conducting legal proceedings and different codes of conduct.

Preparing the baby's room often has a different meaning for this group of adopters. They do not always prepare a room before the child arrives in their country. After all, it can remain unclear as to whether the adoption will be approved right up to the moment the case comes to court.

The general procurement and organisation of the necessary documents at home and abroad is a task for which the DIY adopters are responsible independently of the adoption agency. The adoption agency simply grants its approval to the IND (Immigration and Naturalisation Department) in order to prepare the entry clearance papers for the Netherlands. This is done through the embassy in the country of adoption. The independent adopters will have to prepare piles of paperwork themselves for the rest of the procedure.

The adoption period is a long journey. But so is the unhappy period of medical intervention which most couples go through before they decide to adopt. The good news about adoption is that you are more certain to succeed.

It may be a long journey with unexpected twists and turns and obstacles and diversions, but the child will come!

What is stress?

The phenomenon of stress was first used in the thirties by an Austrian endocrinologist called Selye. He took the term from the English expression stress and strain. Before he realised that the word strain expressed the concept better, the word stress had already become established in society.

Yet whether you use the word stress or strain, the fact remains that the tension or pressure that someone feels is a purely individual feeling. Feelings of stress cannot be generalised, they are directly related to the person and the specific moment.

I like to use the word stress to combine the ideas of tension and pressure. There are positive and negative types of stress. Positive stress is healthy and gives you positive strength, whereas negative stress wears you down and causes blockages in your energy flow.

When is a person under stress, or rather, when does a person feel stressed? What causes stress? The American psychiatrist Holmes examined the relationship between negative stress (excessive pressure) and the emergence of particular symptoms. He developed the so-called Social Readjustment Rating Scale, or SRRS scale, which enabled people to see the extent to which different events in their life give rise to a certain degree of stress, both positive and negative. Events ranged from the birth of a child to the death of a parent. He based his observations on a period of one year and concluded that the amount of positive and negative stress is decisive for the amount of energy we expend on the events causing that stress. The more energy we lose to stress, the more vulnerable we are to side effects and disease.

This is part of Holmes's stress list:

Death of partner	100
Divorce	73

Imprisonment	63
Death of family member	63
Physical injury or disease	53
Marriage	50
Dismissal	47
Reconciliation with partner	45
Disease of family member	44
Pregnancy	40
Sexual problems	39
A new business	39
Change in financial situation	38
Death of a good friend	37
New job	36
Marriage rows	36
High debts	31
Increased responsibility at work	29
Reduced responsibility at work	29
Problems with in-laws	29
Special personal performance	28
Partner returns to work or stops work	26
First day at school or exams	26
General change in life circumstances	25
Problems with superiors	24
Change in personal habits	24
Different working hours or working conditions	20
Moving house	20
New school	19
Different hobbies	19
Change of church activities	19
Change in social activities	18
Small loans	17
Changed sleeping habits	15

Holiday	13
Christmas time	12
Minor violations of the law	11

The risk of physical of psychic symptoms remains fairly low up to 200 points. Remain alert, however, because one still uses up a lot of energy.

Scoring between 200 and 300 points gives a person a 30% higher chance of developing symptoms.

It has been shown that a score of above 300 stress points within twelve months leaves 90% of people particularly susceptible to illness.

Looking at this list, it becomes clear why a long adoption procedure makes you particularly vulnerable to stress. Adoption does not feature in the list, but would certainly score between 50 and 60 points. That means that little else needs to happen to bring you up to 100 points (holiday and Christmas together amount to 25 and are hard to avoid). Due to the length of the period, other stress factors can easily arise. In our case, we had to deal with a whole range of different stress stimulants: the first adoption period, Mette's arrival (birth), my father's death, the second adoption period, which began when we first met Wisse, the uncertainty about Wisse's health, the deaths of several dear people in our family and circle of friends – and so the list steadily grew, not even counting holidays and Christmas. Together with your partner, have a look to see how relevant the list is for your own situation. A high score means you must take better care of yourself and each other.

It is important to realise that a host of systems in your body are activated when you are subjected to stress over a longer period of time. Here are some of the physical changes that take place:

- Rise in blood pressure
- Contraction of blood vessels
- Diminished oxygen levels in body cells

- Therefore, diminished oxygen levels in the brain.
- Accelerated heart rate
- Accelerated breathing
- Rise in cholesterol levels
- Increased production of stomac acid

… and the list continues.

These symptoms can lead to numerous complaints related to cardiac and vascular diseases, stomach and intestinal problems and a general weakening of the auto-immune system.

Due to the release of the substance adrenaline, stress can even have an addictive effect, producing the workaholic who "goes mad" from sitting still when on holiday. He experiences withdrawal from the customary amount of stress and the accompanying adrenaline. Even more common are stories of people who have serious physical problems while on holiday. The sudden death of Dutch TV-personality Willem Ruis is often quoted in this context: working extremely hard and under a great deal of stress, followed by an unexpected death while on holiday.

But it is unlikely to come to that. Remember: you are in charge. Learn to recognise the stress you experience and be conscious of how you deal with it.

Stress during the adoption procedure

'I felt like I was swimming against the current from the first day onwards, as if I was dealing with a policy to systematically put people off adopting. It takes up so much energy that you have none left for other things in life'.

Things that cause stress tend to be precisely those things over which one has little or no control. For most people, the ability to accept loss of control is a less-developed quality, yet this plays a significant role during the adoption procedure.

The survey I carried out among adoptive parents as part of my training as stress consultant, had participants completing a questionnaire in which they used a scale to indicate how much stress they had experienced at certain moments during the whole procedure.

I made a partial distinction between independent adoptive parents and people adopting through an adoption agency.

The differences were quite clear, but the similarities between the two groups even clearer. These are some striking examples of what caused them stress:

For the group adopting through an agency:
- The interview with the adoption agency
- Waiting for the adoption agency to send its proposal
- The journey to the country to pick up the child
- Returning home

For the group of independent adoptive parents:
- Maintaining contacts abroad
- Organising matters abroad
- Court proceedings abroad

Less stress was caused by:
- The decision to adopt
- The VIA course
- The meetings with the Child Protection Agency
- The financial consequences.

To summarise the greatest stress factors:
For the group adopting through an agency, it is the time spent waiting.
For the independent adopters, it is the time spent struggling to conquer obstacles.

Understandably, for the first group loss of control manifests itself passively. After a meeting with the agency, a couple may no longer feel involved in the developments and compelled to wait patiently. I can honestly say that I sometimes longed for such a feeling when we received yet another e-mail from Kenya saying things were not going according to plan. On the other hand, waiting is difficult for adoptive parents-to-be. The drawn-out, unpleasant medical procedures which often precede adoption can turn these people into real fighters. You want nothing more than a child and you have to do more and more in order to get one. That makes these people particularly active, and for active people there is nothing worse than having to passively sit and wait. So when they find themselves having to do just that, their natural tendency to take initiative can prove extremely trying.

For independent adopters, often the continuing struggle with a foreign bureaucratic culture, usually from a distance causes the stress to break out again and again. It is true that it feels as if you are exerting control, but it is an illusory control. You are still dependent as you keep checking up on the authorities, especially the less transparent ones.

For both groups, fear is the underlying feeling to which these feelings of stress can be traced back. In our case, such moments were particularly clear.

Two examples we experienced as extremely stressful, and two, looking back, were much less stressful.

First major example
The judge initially refused to grant the adoption order for Wisse. Until the moment his decision was announced, we had experienced the stress as bearable. There were certainly plenty of things that caused us annoyance to some extent, but this was adoption, after all. We thought we had prepared everything well, even better than with Mette when there had been no Kenyan Child Protection Agency peeping over our shoulders. When the adoption was refused that day, we plunged into feelings of panic and stress. The underlying feeling was the fear that the entire adoption process would come to nothing and we would not be able to adopt Wisse.

Second major example
Back in the Netherlands, we received the news that Wisse would have to leave the country. We were both in the process of regaining our emotional strength after a few tumultuous years and thought we had finally left the stress behind us. We were not prepared for any new shocks, so when the letter announcing the forthcoming deportation procedure arrived, our world collapsed. The underlying feeling was once again fear: the fear that Wisse would be taken away from us due to the arbitrary nature of the bureaucratic situation.

First minor example
Having to wait endlessly for the lawyer at every appointment, always fearing that she might not show up at all and that we would lose precious time in the procedure. No insurmountable problem, but certainly extremely irritating. You have no control over the situation, but after repeatedly experiencing the same thing you start to prepare yourself for a long period of waiting. The fear expressed itself in anger.

Second minor example
We suddenly had to go to Kenya without delay for an appointment with the local Child Protection Agency. We had little time to prepare, yet a lot depended on the meeting. We were worried that the lady conducting the interview might not grant her approval, but in the end the meeting turned out to be extremely positive. A short impulse of stress.

Faced with the examples above, we could have asked ourselves "what if….?" questions:
- What if we were not able to adopt Wisse?
- What if Wisse had to go back to Kenya?
- What if the lawyer did not show up?
- What if the Child Protection Agency denied us approval?

To what extent were these scenarios disastrous and what alternatives were there? The moment you feel paralysed by stress, you can easily lose the creativity needed for viewing a problem from a different perspective.

Ask yourself the question: "What if…?"

See if you can look at a problem creatively to find alternative solutions. Many of you will have asked yourselves and your partners: "What if we really ended up having no children?" I realise that such a question can bring tears to your eyes. But look at the question carefully and listen to your own answer. Then ask yourself other questions. What if I were not healthy, if I had a chronic illness, no legs, he was blind or deaf? What if I had no partner, no parents, no family? What if I had not been born in the Netherlands, but in the slums of Rio de Janeiro?

We were eventually able to look at our own "what if" questions creatively and find alternative courses of action.

We would go and live in Kenya and complete the adoption procedure under Kenyan law.

We would go and live in Kenya or take to the streets and demonstrate in the Netherlands.

We would wait on the lawyer's doorstep the following week.

We would apply for another assessment.

Can you face addressing your own "what if" questions? Where does your creativity lie? If it is snowed under by stress, take a look further on in the book at the possibilities for looking at stress in a different light.

Adoption versus pregnancy

'A natural pregnancy has you feeling the child from day one and the love for that child grows continually. At birth, there is the immediate recognition that it's part of you. People's reactions to the news that we were pregnant were so predictable, unlike the reactions to our announcement that we were also going to adopt, which could sometimes be quite negative.'

'The big difference for me is that with a pregnancy you feel your child growing and therefore establish a bond with the child. It moves when you speak. Once it was out, it didn't feel quite so familiar. I really had to get used to it. Also, you have it with you constantly right after the birth, and it grows up with you. With regard to the health of the baby, there's more tension with a pregnancy. When adopting, you ask for a 'healthy child' or one with an 'operable handicap'. You know more or less what you're going to get.'

'There's not much fun in the period leading up to an adoption, it costs far more money and the process is a long hard slog.'

'I have experience with both. In my opinion, one big difference is the very conscious way in which you deal with the period leading up to the expansion of your family through adoption. Being pregnant is wonderful, especially for a woman, but adoption is more something you experience as a couple, from the very first moment.'

For the majority of couples who adopt, adoption is a last resort for starting a family, of having a child. Between eighty-five and ninety per cent of people who register for adoption have had extensive fertility treatment and have either never been able to have children the natural way or have succeeded in having one or more children but find themselves unable to have any more. Pregnancy was the dream, adoption is now reality and thus the new dream.

An adoption can of course be viewed as a special kind of pregnancy. The two share common ground, as both produce a child. But there are many differences we generally tend to overlook.

First of all, the roles are divided differently. Adoption creates total equality between the two parents. All steps are taken together, although they may be experienced differently. The first obvious step is the compulsory VIA information course. You *have* to go there together. Many men experience this equality as particularly positive during the adoption procedure. They are either actively or passively involved in this form of pregnancy in the same way as the woman is. Not one of the two partners is doing all the work. Joint action is extremely important. In case of a pregnancy, a man more or less stands on the sidelines and watches his partner become heavier, carry his child inside her day and night, feel it move, and cope with the discomfort. A man can put his hand on his partner's belly and feel the baby kick, but he remains a bit of an outsider.

Men therefore feel more equality throughout the experience of adoption. They like to be in control of things and this is easier with an adoption than with a pregnancy. Let a man act and he is at his best. A man gets restless from too much waiting, especially waiting without a clear end in sight. He fares well making beds and shelves, wallpapering bedrooms and choosing cupboards. The woman then picks the clothes, fills the cupboards and makes the bed. This may sound rather clichéd, but in my wide circle of friends and relatives I have seen it again and again: a 'natural' balance between active and passive.

Every person carries reserves of active and passive energy. One day's balance may well differ from the next. But balance is important to be able to function to the best of one's abilities and to feel good being oneself.

Every adoption procedure disrupts this balance of active and passive energy, however positive the experience may feel for a man. After the active start for both partners when registering for adoption, a long period of waiting follows before anything else happens at all (as I said earlier, the situation in 2006 is that an average of 22 months passes before the VIA course can begin). Then comes the active period of information, talks with the Child Protection Agency and adoption agency, which again are followed by, in many cases, several years of waiting before your child arrives. This apparent helpless waiting for the fulfilment of your ultimate wish in life throws the balance between active and passive energy into utter turmoil.

The imbalance may be experienced differently by the two partners. Same-sex partners also often experience an emotional division of roles whereby one of the partners fits into the passive role and the other into the active. It is not a static process. When I look at myself, I often feel most at home in the active role, but from one moment to the next can enjoy simply 'being' and not having to do anything. Energy is in motion, hence you can get up feeling tired and apathetic one morning, then feel the sky is the limit after a stimulating phone call. Or it can happen the other way round. Energy *has* to be in motion, otherwise blockages develop. This is another risk in such a long-winded procedure: getting stuck in that passive, powerless feeling. All kinds of physical symptoms may develop as the waiting leads to tension causing tiredness, headaches, disturbed sleeping and eating patterns, emotional imbalance, et cetera.

For independent adopters, another imbalance often lies in wait. Independent adopters often have an affinity with a particular country, or an orphanage or person in a country with which no contract has been established by the Ministry of Justice. An adoption from a so-called non-contract country is possible, but has to be organised entirely by the independent adopters. This often involves all the procedures, court proceedings and bureaucracy before the case is finalised. A Dutch adoption agency acting as partial mediator checks the reliability of the contact in all cases, after which authorisation is given to start the procedure for that particular child. This precaution is of course taken to prevent child trafficking.

So for independent adopters, the imbalance is often on a different level. They have to pull out all the stops to get the foreign bureaucracy moving and keep it going. Weekly, if not daily, they are ready to deal with more unexpected events. A lot of action is required of them and they have very little time and opportunity to wait passively for things to happen.

'I was so busy gathering documents, getting things stamped, visiting embassies, organising translations and so on, that I didn't have any time to wait. Together with another prospective adoptive mother, I drove so many miles in my car that we didn't even have time to decorate the baby's room. Two weeks before we set off to collect our children we had to make a start on it.'

When such people get caught up in too much activity without unwinding, a variety of symptoms may emerge, but in the heat of the moment it is tempting not to feel or notice them. Symptoms include irritability, headaches, disturbed sleep, constant alertness, increased muscle tension, weight loss, etc.

When I look back on our adoption period as independent adopters, I realise that while we were in the middle of it all I thought I had everything under control. But I was actually seeing a doctor for a sleeping disorder that I attributed to my irregular working hours, visiting the acupuncturist for headaches and the shiatsu therapist for muscle pains, taking Bach flower remedies for irritability and became almost aggressive in the supermarket if they did not have a product I thought I needed. In hindsight, it appears I was no different from other independent adoptive parents. I *thought* I was managing it all wonderfully.

And that is one of the dangers of this period. Being wrapped up in something you want so badly that you cannot or do not want to feel the pain, sadness and anger. You *think* that you are doing well, but in reality you are not facing the pain of the anger and sadness you feel. You think that you are living in balance, although it may be a very fine line that you are treading that is keeping you from falling off the edge.

Relationship under pressure?

'After 17 years I've realised that the basis for a good relationship is talking to each other.'

There is a very real possibility that during the long adoption period, a couple will experience moments when conversation dries up. At a certain moment, you may misunderstand each other. It is even possible that you seem to lose each other somewhere along the way.

This is hardly a desirable state of affairs. After all, you are in it together and grappling with the same problems.

A possible cause of an impasse is not being able to reach each other anymore and failing to meet on the same level of verbal and non-verbal communication. Library and bookshelves are filled with books about communication in both the workand the domestic sphere. As everyone has his or her own unique way of communicating and often takes it for granted that the other person will understand this unique way of communicating in both the work and the domestic sphere. When an external source of constant pressure is intruding on the relationship, which is the case during the adoption period, communication can become disturbed and sometimes even cease altogether. This is dangerous, because a couple needs each other during this mammoth pregnancy and even more so afterwards. Friends of ours once said: only think of having children if the relationship is good, because it will not get any better once the children arrive. And as far as I can judge, they have a wonderful relationship and three children. We would never put it in such extreme terms, but it is true that as well as adding a wonderful new dimension to your relationship, having children also brings a certain element of disruption.

So the essential thing is to find each other and keep hold of each other, as advocated in the marriage vow: "To have and to hold."

How to manage this.
- It is essential to realise that men and women communicate with each other differently and deal with things differently. This need not be a problem; it is simply a fact. Accepting this fact requires that you:

- Let go of any prejudice about your partner
- Give up wanting to change the other person
- Accept yourself as you are
- Accept your partner as he or she is
- Examine your relationship carefully

How do you communicate with each other? Read on to find other points you may recognise from your own relationship.

Given that as a man and a woman you are different from each other and deal differently with the things that cross your path, it can be expected that you will have different ways of dealing with the stress caused by adoption.

Men have the natural tendency to withdraw into themselves when faced with great problems. This can take the form of going upstairs and sitting at the computer or taking themselves to the gym. Or they may just not react when spoken to. They do not do this deliberately, it is in their nature, and if they are given room to react this way, they feel better for it in the end. Men look at problems from various angles and will approach you on the matter when they are ready to talk to you about it.

Women, on the other hand, do not want to withdraw into themselves in the face of great problems, they want to talk about them. Above all with their partners, especially in the case of adoption problems, but also perhaps with relatives, friends or fellow-sufferers. In this way, they try to put the problem into perspective and determine a role for themselves. Perhaps they vent their emotions more than they actually solve the problem, but it creates the circumstances they need within which they can find a solution. They feel better for it afterwards.

If you recognise this difference in your relationship, you may be able to find a way of respecting each other's method of solving problems. My husband and I also found a way of making problems subjects of discussion, with varying degrees of success. I had to learn to leave him in peace and he had to learn to listen to my endless tirades (or at least pretend to). Whenever we bungled something, we ended up laughing about it together, precisely because we seemed to have forgotten what we had learned about how to communicate with each other.

Men and women differ on many fronts of course, as you will have noticed yourself. Reading maps, asking for help, setting priorities, driving cars, etc. Another well-known fact is that men can often only focus on one thing at a time.

If there is a great problem, such as adoption stress, a man, being able to concentrate on only one thing at a time, will give his all to the problem with the intention of solving it. Other things will then pale into insignificance and you should not bother him with them. He has his own list of priorities and so it might happen that he forgets your birthday or anniversary. This is not ill-will. He is thoroughly wrapped up in finding a solution to his problem.

When a woman encounters a problem, she can really lose control. She is no heroine when it comes to setting priorities and can become overwhelmed by all the things that cross her path. As she remains capable of focusing on many things at once, it is possible that her emotions are not only determined by the adoption stress.

With stress during the adoption procedure, a man will thus tend to tackle the factor causing the stress in the attempt to make the stress disappear. He looks at the problem as objectively as possible and immediately sets about trying to solve it. A woman in times of stress, especially over such a long period, looks at the matter subjectively and listens to her inner feelings. She perceives several problems at once, and will attempt to work out what means she has at her disposal to protect her inner self. Similar to how it was long ago: men went out hunting to kill prey, and women gathered useful objects while waiting.

Some days when all hope would leave me, I would feel overpowered by the hardship, the disappointment. It was at those moments that I had to let it out somehow, find comfort, visit a friend or two, have an espresso, go shopping, take a bath – in short, I felt better when I "gathered" pleasant objects or experiences. Whenever I opened my troubled mind to my husband, I had to take care not to give him the impression that I expected him to solve things for me. Many of the problems had no direct solution anyway, it was more a question of dealing with the frustration of waiting and the feeling of being manipulated. As we had both looked into the subject of how differently men and women deal with their lives, such situations usually ended well. I advise others to read one or more books on the subject. The intention is certainly not to categorise men and women. For example, I have plenty of male aspects in me with regard to emotions and how to deal with them. The intention is to respect each other's differences. When a man withdraws emotionally, the two of you can laugh about it later when he has come back. This strategy certainly increased our enjoyment of each other. It strengthened our relationship, which was just what we needed in this special period.

In summary:
Bear in mind that this *may* be normal behaviour for men under stress:
- He withdraws into himself. Communication temporarily ceases.
- He becomes irritable if he is not given the chance to withdraw.
- He shuts himself off if he is not allowed to be irritable (he defends his space).

Bear in mind that this *may* be normal behaviour for women under stress:
- She feels overwhelmed by stress; a straw can break a camel's back.
- She feels tense when the partner does not listen.
- She feels exhausted and hollow.

It is therefore well possible that women complain of fatigue during and after an adoption period. This can be largely overcome if you work consciously to maintain the best possible communication and remain alert to good stress control.

Leave a man in peace and allow him space when he asks for it (even non-verbally); let a woman talk; cherish her, even if she does not specifically ask you to.

Adoption is all about communication.

Emotions

Every day, we experience an endless expression of emotions. We feel disappointed, let down, irritated, cheerful, or we can be afraid to give in to certain feelings – complete the list yourself for today or yesterday or last week.

Despite the apparent multitude of feelings, they can essentially be reduced to four basic emotions:

Fear
Anger
Sadness
Happiness

Whatever emotion you are experiencing, you will find it fits into one of these categories if you trace it back to its original form.

During exceptional periods in your life you will encounter a whole scale of emotions. Adoption is such a period in which you are particularly emotional and vulnerable over a longer period of time. Sometimes your own flow of energy has almost run dry, making you receptive to the energy of others. This is a good moment to think carefully about the most draining emotions you are experiencing and why they are emerging in this period of your life.

If you feel one of these strong emotions, use the RET technique (see chapter 'Letting go and finding a new way forward') to help you identify what is feeding this feeling. This may help you deal with the emotion more effectively.

This chapter includes short accounts of the experiences of other adoptive parents to illustrate my points. The parents-to-be remain anonymous for their protection; some of them are still in the throes of their adoption procedure.

Fear

> *'Sometimes things were taking far too long and I started to worry: what if she falls ill before we can go and collect her. I was really nervous in the last few weeks before our journey, kept getting infections, couldn't sleep and was very tense…'*

(independent adopter with one natural child)

> *'Of course all kinds of things can go wrong when you're pregnant, too, but at least there's a beginning and an end to it and it lasts nine months at most. The adoption period is riddled with uncertainty: will we be approved as parents or not, will the judge grant the adoption or not, will we get her papers or not, how long will it all take… You feel all sorts of things as a mother during the pregnancy and can even exert some influence over how you feel. During the adoption period, you miss a lot of what's going on and you're often plagued by the fear of whether it will all turn out well. You have so little to really hold on to.'*

Fear is a deep-rooted feeling in the heart of many prospective adoptive parents, whether they are fully aware of it or not. After all, the majority of hopeful would-be adopters have already experienced years of medical interventions and a constant feeling of uncertainty: the fear of the latest attempt failing again. This fear seems to be confirmed by the reality of being childless against one's will and having to accept repeated failed attempts.

During the adoption period, these feelings of fear initially appear to fade into the background. However, as the waiting time drags on and the procedure abroad proves more difficult than foreseen, the feelings of uncertainty and fear resurface.

Talking about these feelings of fear can help neutralise the experience and get things back into perspective. However, fellow sufferers are not always readily available for sharing one's experiences. It is no coincidence that in the Netherlands many groups of people sharing all kinds of problems regularly meet to address their feelings of fear, uncertainty and sadness.

If fear is on one end of the emotional scale, trust is on the other, which could explain why the stress factor among independent adopters is so high during the court proceedings abroad. After all, you have to trust a legal system which is unfamiliar to you in a country where you are only a visitor. It is almost impossible. People who have an agency organise their adoption trust that the organisation will be functioning well in the country of adoption. In their case it is usually the length of the waiting time that undermines their trust. Both groups are vulnerable to fear due to their history of having their fears confirmed (it is as I feared: I cannot have children). During such long periods of waiting, irrational ideas have every chance of gaining the upper hand.

For some couples, the age limit also plays a role throughout the waiting period. If there may be no more than forty years age difference between the eldest adoptive parent and the child upon its arrival in the country, this can turn into a painful factor as the years pass and the uncertainty intensifies as to whether they will be able to adopt a baby. This is a deep wish for many prospective adoptive parents, as the bonding process with a baby is often easier than with older children, some of whom may have been neglected in orphanages for many years.

Anger

'The moments of frustration and stress are countless. Even without including reactions from people around you. As soon as you decide to adopt, everyone thinks they can interfere and give their opinion, whether you asked for it or not, and however hurtful it might be. The underlying idea is: if you can't have any children yourself you are not

in a position to demand anything... Most of my complaints and angry feelings are aimed at the Ministry of Justice (though I never let them get out of hand, as we are in a most unpleasant position of dependency). The simple fact that such an intimate process like the creation of your family should be taken right out of your hands and the fact that you find yourself being dictated from all sides, is harsh.'

'I got really angry about repeatedly having to explain why we wanted to adopt. Having a child the natural way is totally normal, but when you want to adopt everyone wants to know why. You are asked most intimate questions. I had very negative experiences filling in those questionnaires from all sorts of authorities during the adoption procedure, which I felt were an invasion of my privacy.'

'I found my employer's uncooperative attitude when I had to take three months' leave to complete the adoption period in our child's native country, very disheartening. I had been under the illusion that everyone was supporting us, but that was certainly not the case'.

'Of course you ask yourself: why do I have to bear my all when two streets down an antisocial family has one baby after the other with no one allowed to say a word about it?'

Almost all adoptive couples are confronted with feelings of anger. The problem is that there is not much one can really do to address their immediate cause. After all, getting upset with the judge, lawyer, Child Protection Agency, adoption agency or whatever other authority could be dangerous as it might have a negative effect on the progress of the adoption procedure.

There does not always have to be an immediate cause for such anger. Simply feeling totally powerless can be enough to cause a deep feeling of anger.

Getting angry with the legal powers abroad may have even more far-reaching consequences. It is often more advisable to stay polite and adapt to the speed and style of the country in which the adoption is taking place, even if you find yourself gritting your teeth at your end of the telephone or in the umpteenth office. This anger, too, need not be rational. Other countries may simply apply different rules and regulations and have a culture with which we do not automatically know how to deal at home. Who abroad knows the ins and outs of our legislation and legal system, anyway? Who determines what is just? Are you getting angry because your sense of justice and honesty is not being honoured? Are you getting angry because what you want is not happening?

In all cases, we are dealing with feelings of anger, often coupled with powerlessness, ultimately based on the fear that it will all go wrong yet again.

And yet, these feelings of anger and frustration have to go somewhere. The most obvious direction is generally the partner, work or friends, or it is channelled inwards and causes physical symptoms such as headaches, tiredness, sleeplessness, etc.

Anger is an explosive energy that must find a way out. If you do something with it and do not let it get you down, it can inspire you and energise you. If you do nothing with it, a block forms and the feelings will come out at a later date. Postponing the expression of anger has rarely caused people any joy.

Are you to stand there and stamp your feet or throw crockery around the kitchen? Probably not. Look for a method which suits you (in my case I put music on at full volume and danced around like a madwoman, and now that I have the children, it can be quite fun, even if I am angry at them). Channel your anger. Practising sports is also a tried and tested method for letting out pent-up energy. A tennis ball can take a lot.

Sadness

'The medical procedures were terrible, so much hope and pushing your limits every time, staying positive while others around you got pregnant. Being around babies was very depressing.'

'After the birth and burial of our little baby we talked intensely for three weeks about a future with or without children, about a pregnancy with the medical risk of another stillborn… but we knew one thing for sure: we wanted children… In view of our age we registered with the Ministry of Justice immediately although we were not entirely sure at that moment if we really wanted to go through with it. But we told ourselves: when we are done mourning, we can still decide if we want to proceed with the adoption or not, but at least the process will be under way.'

'She sat there alone on a large chair with a blanket around her. We were shocked: she was so small. I picked her up and she hardly reacted… Our guide repeatedly tried to establish contact with her but in vain… On the third day of our stay, we got a phone call from the adoption agency saying that a CT scan would have to be done of her head. After I hang up I knew that all was not well with our little girl. We cried our eyes out… After the scan, the results were discussed. We were advised not to adopt this child. As adoptive parents, we had to decide on the spot whether we wanted to take her with us… The main reason for us not to take her was that in view of her brain damage, we would never be able to establish a bond with her. But it still hurts terribly that we had to leave her behind. She will always have a special place in our heart.'

We have already examined sadness. Look critically at yourself and decide whether you have worked through pain from the past. Check if those 'drawers' are empty.

Bear in mind that during the adoption procedure you often have unbridled supplies of energy which cause emotions to get snowed under. This is due to the 'drive' that adoptive parents experience, enabling them to take on excessive pressure. This pressure comes in the guise of waiting and struggling against the obstacles and disappointments, not just once, but again and again. The drive comes from the fact that you have your eyes firmly fixed on long-term happiness: a child for life. A person will make great sacrifices for life-long happiness. Many emotions are pushed aside during the adoption procedure. The risk however, is that rubbish that is pushed out of sight will not get cleared away by the dustmen.

A situation whereby the child arrives and the parents are tripping over their own rubbish must not be allowed. So cleansing is the answer.

Disappointment = pain

This is what Kahlil Gibran says about pain in *The Prophet*:

> *And could you keep your heart in wonder at the daily miracles of your life, your pain would not seem less wondrous than your joy; And you would accept the seasons of your heart, even as you have always accepted the seasons that pass over your fields. And you would watch with serenity through the winters of your grief.*

Every disappointment causes pain. Sometimes just a little, sometimes a great deal. The degree of pain you feel is not necessarily proportionate to the size of the disappointment. The extent to which one feels pain differs from one person to the next, and from one moment to the next in a day or in your life. When you are older, you may look back on a failed teenage love affair and smile, but some people never get over such heartache.

During the adoption period, you may well be confronted with disappointments both great and small. It is not certain that they will happen, but it is likely. That phone call you have been waiting for for weeks may not come, and the proposal you receive may not match your dream, either will cause you disappointment and pain. The judge in the adoptive country may refuse to grant the adoption, causing a major disappointment and great pain.

The danger of pain in this period is that it seems subordinate to the ultimate aim: a child. How much pain do you want to feel about a failed telephone call, a disappointing message, an amended law which leaves you waiting even longer for the child whose photo is already on your mantelpiece? How much pain will you let in before your soul hardens?

It is worth recognising the benefit of pain. An everyday example: everyone knows that when you burn yourself on something, you have to cool the burned area. You then apply ointment or a plaster to protect the area from another 'trauma'. You acknowledge the pain, recognise the cause, tend to the injury and remember to learn from it. Pain is meant to be addressed in some way, not for you to thoughtlessly or consciously hide. Personally, I was stimulated by the disappointments and pain of the adoption period. I took them head-on the hard way and fought my way through to a new way, a new possibility. Pain was certainly not something that was going to hold me back – on the contrary, it made me even more determined to persevere. As I avoided acknowledging the purpose of pain, the blisters most probably formed ugly scars that I may still carry in places today. There was certainly no shortage of pain or disappointments of all magnitudes. Yet I did not see the pain's purpose. What happened was that the disappointments faded, sometimes to be replaced by new ones, sometimes because other things happened which pushed the feeling of disappointment into the background. The pain that resulted from the disappointment did not fade, did not become any less intense – it just went into hiding. Sometimes, it flamed up unexpectedly and took the form of a crying fit, an outburst unrelated to reality, or just a general feeling of depression without my being able to identify the cause. This is what pent-up pain does. It has to come out, be named, be analysed, so that from the moment of acknowledgement, it can evolve into something that can be accepted, as Kahlil Gibran so eloquently says.

Of course, I also know that disappointments are a part of life, so you do not need to make a big drama out of them. But you should not forget that you are particularly vulnerable during an adoption procedure. A woman may still be recovering from the enormous load of chemical hormones she was given when attempting to conceive. She is also vulnerable because she is living in a state of continuous tension. Consider the adoption period as a bow without the arrow. You do not know how big the bow is or how long the cord, or even how long the tension has been there. As I said before, you do not always feel the long-term pain or you consider it a positive experience, but it makes you vulnerable to disappointments and therefore, to pain.

So, what types of disappointments may one encounter? And more importantly, how should one deal with them?

Due to the length of the adoption period, which will always take several years, the range of disappointments can be particularly complex. In a previous chapter we have already come across the SRRS scale which identifies the major changes in one's life. This chapter deals with disappointments rather than changes, although in some cases the two overlap.

Examples of disappointments during the adoption procedure:
- The date for travelling to collect the child is postponed.
- You are allocated a child of one and a half instead of a baby.
- The judge in the country from which you plan to adopt is on summer holidays.
- An epidemic breaks out in the home country of your future adoptive child and you cannot travel there to collect the child.
- The lawyer working for you turns out to be unreliable.
- You have an unpleasant meeting with the Child Protection Agency.
- The child turns out to have a minor handicap.
- You have the feeling that the procedure is not moving forward.
- Every day, you wait in vain for the phone call to tell you that your child may be collected.

Every disappointment has a unique impact. The greatest disappointment would be not being able to adopt a child, and fortunately that very rarely happens. All other setbacks seem secondary, but in fact they are not. And finally, we are often confronted with losing control over 'our' business.

As well as adoption-related disappointments there are the disappointments of everyday life. But as I mentioned before, you are often all the more sensitive to this category:
- A friend does not call to ask how you are both doing.
- Your birthday is forgotten at work.

- Your partner forgets your wedding anniversary.
- You and your partner have not had a free evening together in two weeks.
- He still has not read the book you recommended him.
- The restaurant you had picked for dinner is closed that evening.
- The high-pressure sprayer fails to work when you want to hose down the drive.

Your disappointment needs care and compensation, like the blister in the earlier example. If you do not tend to it, it will go from bad to worse. This is no happy state of affairs, because apart from these relatively small disappointments, there are the larger, more significant ones, as well.

The following exercise helps to give you insight into your way of dealing with disappointments:

Think back on your life and choose a moment when you experienced physical pain. Maybe you had a fall when skiing, banged into a glass door, cut yourself while cooking, burned yourself – any kind of accident. Look back on the event and try to recall how you dealt with it. Are you someone who needs a lot of attention, feels ashamed, gets angry or blames someone else? Or do you perhaps tend to spoil yourself, be hard on yourself or make fun of yourself? The exercise is most effective if you use several examples and write down your reactions. As you look back on how you dealt with this pain, try to see yourself truthfully and decide whether your method was desirable and if there is an alternative method you could have used.

Now make the transition to the present and project current, non-physical pain. If you deal with it in a similar way, see if you can use the same alternative. If you are hard on yourself, try to make up for a disappointment with a loving gesture, or, if you find this difficult, look for someone from whom you can receive love. If anger is your form of expression, make sure that instead of getting stuck in that method you find an activity in which you can expend your anger. It is highly likely that you will find a pattern that you have been using to deal with disappointments for years. Look closely at whether your method is desirable, and try to find a creative solution, preferably with your partner.

If you have discovered an undesirable pattern, there is room to introduce change. You are never too old to change something about yourself, especially not if you are being supported by your partner. It takes courage to tend to your pain in such a way that it brings you composure and balance – that serenity to which Kahlil Gibran refers – but these will prove invaluable assets to help you through the adoption period.

Disappointment = sadness

The majority of adoptive parents are experts in coping with sadness. After all, the decision to adopt was often preceded by a long period of trying to beat involuntary childlessness. And there is no joy in the procedures this involves. By the time we started our adoption procedure, I had started to put all that behind me (four laparoscopies, one cyst removal, a number of courses of medication which induced a chemical menopause, all examinations performed twice as the gynaecologist wanted to have the latest data when I married for the second time, four IUIs and four IVFs spread over ten years), but I cried like a child when a friend's attempts at IUI failed again. This was of course for their sadness, but my own old pain also came rising to the surface again. When have you finished working through your sadness – or when is it time to start doing so?

First, one has to acknowledge sadness. This relates to how you yourself deal with things that happen to you. You cannot measure sadness, it is not a scientific subject. Each experience of sadness is different from the last, and everyone experiences sadness in their own way. Even extremely intense sadness such as the death of a parent is experienced and expressed differently by each child in the family. The same applies to the sadness you encounter during the adoption period.

Pain is closely linked with sadness. A disappointment can cause both. Pain can be seen as the direct wound, for example the blister after the burn. Sadness is the feeling that the pain can cause, for example when an ugly scar remains. This makes sadness so unique. One person may not be bothered at all by the scar, whereas another might lose sleep over it. How you deal with sadness has a lot to do with how you look at yourself. I discuss this further in a later chapter on mourning.

What goes for everyone is the fact that sadness should not be stowed away. It does not help. Sadness is always connected with saying goodbye to something that meant a lot to you. This may be the date on which you had hoped to travel to collect your child, the good impression you had of the lawyer who was to organise your adoption abroad or the dream image of the little baby you thought you were going to adopt. But also the wish to be able to carry a child inside you or the warmth of a friend during the long and difficult years of hospital visits. Even not winning the lottery carries a moment of saying goodbye. Saying goodbye to the dream of a million.

Prospective adoptive parents, you, the readers of this book, know all about saying goodbye. Each month you experienced the sadness of not being pregnant, often for years on end. Every month another mourning process that could take anything from an hour or a week to even face.

Elisabeth Kübler Ross has written a very clear book about mourning processes, saying goodbye and coming to terms with your sadness. In her book *On death and dying* she describes the various stages of mourning. The book is based on the mourning for someone who has died of an incurable disease, but whether we are dealing with a lost competition, a bad mark in geography, the bankruptcy of a company, a stolen purse, a dead mother or an unborn child, the stages of mourning still apply.

In her book, she describes roughly four stages which lead to the final part of the journey one can undertake in the attempt to process mourning, from the moment that you still see yourself as the leading actor in a film to the moment you have the feeling you are watching a film about you.

First stage: denial. It cannot be true, someone has made a mistake, it is not about me/us. At this stage, the whole truth does not yet fully penetrate. One does not comprehend the reality, as if still protecting oneself from the often complex truth so as to let it in at a later stage in small doses. This provides time to prepare oneself for facing the truth.

Second stage: anger. Everyone around you can become a target of your anger, which certainly does not have to be aimed at the real cause of the sadness or disappointment. Slowly but surely, you realise the impact of what you are experiencing. You want to be heard, often unlike the first phase when you might feel withdrawn or shut yourself off. Why me/us? You realise you have lost control over something, and imagine that something or someone has done this to you. Only slowly does the truth dawn on you.

Third stage: bargaining. This is a familiar phenomenon in adoption procedures. The moment you become aware of the disappointment you start looking for escape routes, bargaining over what other possibilities there could be. During those visits to the hospital, too, when you were told there was not much more they could do for you, you still looked for escape routes to get away from the truth that you would not be able to have children the (un)natural way.

Fourth stage: depression, despondency. Deep sadness for what never was. At last you face the fact that what you hoped for will never happen, and a new sadness emerges for having to search a new way. One that you would never have searched for or chosen voluntarily.

The last stage is the actual acceptance.

If on the way towards acceptance you take your time and are surrounded by people who stand by you and care and understand, the moment will come that the film in which you played the leading role changes into the film you are instead merely watching.

The friend or foe called 'hope' wanders about every new development. Hope that you cling on to and that often leads you astray and hinders you in the process of mourning what you have lost. 'Hope lost, everything lost', goes a Dutch saying. But this does not apply to irrational hope. You have to rid yourself of irrational hope in order to be able to move forward in your life.

The different stages that Elisabeth Kübler-Ross describes are not a checklist. The stage of disbelief and numbness does not always set in first, nor is this stage certain not to return once you have already experienced it. The process is one of constant movement until you arrive at the moment of acceptance.

The mourning process of involuntary childlessness is unique. You lose something you never had (a child). You then lose something you had for a very long time but which is no good to you any more (hope). Finally, it is often only years later that you realise you were in the mourning process all along. Yet every month brought renewed hope. There may even have been pregnancies which lasted only a few weeks, or even the full term. But these children could not survive. Sometimes you could at least see the logic of this, which helped you mourn the child. Something tangible. But after eleven years of medical interventions and no second pregnancy, what is there to mourn now?

Do you see your life as one of missed opportunities, personal failure, loss of respect for your own body? How far should you go trying to intervene medically? Where did the mourning process begin, and above all, where does it end?

I had many moments of recognition when I read the book *Eisprong* ('Ovulation') by Judith Uyterlinde. During the years she spent trying to get pregnant. She, too, underwent many mourning processes accompanied by feelings of disbelief, anger and sadness. The most moving part of the book is the ending. After miscarriages, further attempts to get pregnant, determination, perseverance and IVF, she ends her book by asking her husband the question: "Shall we take the plunge again?"

Here is an exercise to give you insight into how you deal with feelings of sadness:

> *Draw the front view of a chest of drawers. You can decide how big and how many drawers but make sure you can write something on each drawer. Write on each of the drawers something that has made you sad. This will of course include adoption-related events, but you can be more general if you like. It is your chest of drawers and you can put in whatever you like. When you have written something on each drawer, take a symbolic look inside one of the drawers to see whether and how you dealt with this sadness.*

How does your approach to the experience of sadness fare when you consider it in the light of the four stages described above? Did you deal with your sadness in such a way that you could actually let it go? As you open the other drawers you will probably find a pattern in the way you have dealt with sadness. Should or could you have dealt with it differently? You are the expert, so you are the one with the answer.

In our personal case there were a lot of these drawers, each containing sad experiences of varying intensities. I have noticed that I run into problems if I do not take time to cry. My parents used to call me a cry baby at home. I hated it when they said that, so I built up my own protection by becoming harder on myself. That worked well for a while until my defences broke down when I was caught off guard, and that is when the tears came. But for me crying has a healing quality. When I forget that, things get bottled up and harden inside me and I find myself making tactless remarks which make both myself and others look ridiculous. Alternatively, the tears could be delayed as they were on the unforgettable day when the judge in Kenya refused to grant Wisse's adoption. Of course I must have heard his pronouncement, but the shock was so great that it did not get through to me. I felt numbed. Then came the incredulity: no, this was a mistake, how could it be possible? I was ready to go back and challenge the judge. I felt anger towards her and started to panic about the possible consequences of the ruling. The tears came later when I was able to grab some moments alone in a bathroom, for we had two little children running around. But there were not enough of these moments and the sadness remained simmering for a long time, even after the adoption was granted a week later.

This experience thus unleashed a wide range of emotions in various forms and in a changing order. It was only much later that I realised I had forgotten to cry, and that I needed to cry at moments of sadness more than I had always thought. It is not childish; it is part of who I am.

For many prospective adoptive parents, the mourning process is the acceptance of one's involuntary childlessness. Each failed attempt was already a mourning process in itself. But once the disbelief, anger and pain finally turn into acceptance and strength, it is possible to continue with everyday life. The hidden danger is that you hoard the sadness away in a drawer and continue to envisage the beautiful child you will one day adopt. This can divert the attention from the drawers which are ajar and which still contain old rubbish. But sadness ignored in a drawer does not wear off. And the greater the number of full or half-full drawers, the greater the danger that the chest will suddenly become too full and topple over. After all, the adoption procedure lasts years, often years during which the sadness related to your childlessness could be compounded by other sad events. You could experience a parent's illness or death, health problems of your own, a divorce in your circle of friends, and so on.

Tidying up those drawers can lead to some real surprises. But if the pain has been tended to, the surprises can be truly wonderful.

Letting go of sadness and pain

Talking about letting go is not the same as not thinking about it anymore. Letting go demands action on the part of the person carrying it out, i.e. you. Letting go only pays off after you have made the investment. When you look at your way of dealing with disappointments, pain and sadness, you will most probably notice a pattern, one which you have likely been following for years. I look at myself and discover that crying, although my parents made fun of it, has healing properties for me which helps me to process my pain and sadness. I used to skip off to infants' school, where I would spend the whole day crying and then skip home again at the end of the day. I had an immense separation anxiety. My mother had just had her second child, my sister, and I had to stay at school all day. Most children in the Netherlands go home for lunch, but the distance to my school was too great, so I stayed there in between morning and afternoon lessons... An element of basic security disappeared and I only got it back much later in life. Crying for me has always been a way to work through my sadness; it is what I am used to. I started thinking about my fear of abandonment and the influence that the loss of a basic feeling of security had on me. I started to put my new insight to work. Thus alerted to the mechanisms at work within me, I can now cope much better with a number of things that may happen to me, such as the loss of a relationship or valuable and much-loved friendships, and I am better able to maintain the feeling of self-confidence that tells me that I am a precious person. But changing takes time.

First, you have to take a good look at what you want to let go of. You first have to hold something firmly in your hands before you can let it go. You have to be able to name it: this is what I have in my hands and this is what I want to let go of.

The primary purpose of human beings is not to change. Research has shown that a large majority of people feel comfortable within set patterns, some more than others, but there is only a small percentage of true adventurers. Most people stay in the area in which they grew up. We look for security and permanence. This often results in making excuses for not changing: "My mother/father was the same" or "I have been doing it this way all my life" and plenty more of such unhelpful comments.

The good news is that you do not have to see it this way. Change is possible, but takes time and energy, as I said before. To break a pattern, you have to integrate the new pattern about 200 times before it sticks. When you want to change a particular thought you may have this may seem rather a lot, but a person has approximately 30,000 to 40,000 thoughts per day, so perhaps it is not so much after all. And there is only one person who can control your thoughts and that is you. The only one to command your powers of thought is you.

Here is an interesting exercise:

Make the decision to take no sugar in coffee or tea two hundred times if you normally take sugar, put the heating on one degree lower two hundred times, ride your bike two hundred times in a higher or lower gear, or eat two hundred meals with the hand you do not normally use, and see what it changes in you and above all how long it takes.

But how can you learn to let go? Having first discovered a pattern in your way of experiencing pain and sadness and realised that it could take time and effort to change that pattern, you are ready to make a start on the process of change. It is important to realise that we have acquired the way we think, often as a form of protection or out of habit. If painful moments or thoughts keep coming back to you in various forms, see them as opportunities for change. We often subconsciously keep emotional memories alive. For example, take a look at a memory such as the shoes you got as a child. A Dutch saying goes: "Do not throw old shoes out before you have new ones", but that does imply that at some point, you should indeed throw those old shoes away. Try to see your emotional memories as shoes that you used to wear but have outgrown. Perhaps as a child your ginger hair was made fun of, but now that you have found someone who loves it as a golden mane you have completely got over it. It can be this way with all pain from the past. You have to set your mind to it and that means having to look at yourself in the mirror again and again and saying to yourself: I do not want this any more, I am going to do things differently. The same as you look at your ginger locks, look at past pain and cherish it as one of life's lessons from which you have emerged a stronger person. Louise Hay writes about letting go in her book *You can heal your life*: "It may be that we have regrets, feel sadness, pain, fear and guilt, reproach ourselves, are angry, harbour resentment or even want to take revenge. We have all these emotional states if we do not want to forgive; if we refuse to let go and experience the present moment".

I had to forgive my parents for something they did and thought was right without realising its implications. For me it was not right. But they were not to know that. How good it was to be able to talk to them about this later and so let go and accept that I am who I am and have to deal with things in a way which is right for me.

Exercise:
> *Take another look inside the chest of drawers. Open one of the drawers, perhaps one with less intense contents, and consider what you could do with it bearing in mind all the emotional states mentioned above. What feelings come to mind when you look at the contents of the drawer? To help you find the answer you could perhaps use a Bach flower remedy. Try it! Feel what effect it has on you and then maybe you will be able to empty the next drawer with more pleasure.*

If you are going to be getting your house ready for new offspring, you might as well take the chance to throw open a few old drawers.

Letting go to go forward

In previous chapters, I talked about pain and how it should be tended to rather than ignored, and sadness and how it must be felt and not hidden, and finally how we can name pain and sadness and then let them go. Three steps to make you feel a whole lot better and save that energy for things that will happen to you tomorrow. How will we deal with them when they happen?

First of all, you have learnt a lot about yourself and perhaps detected a pattern. This is a huge step, and means that you have already benefited more from this intense time than we did during our own adoption period. Due to the length of the procedure and often also the age of the people concerned (as perhaps in your case), confrontation with you own ego, your own identity, may come more quickly, unexpectedly and intensely than for other people your age. Someone from the Child Protection Agency once said in response to an article on stress during the adoption period in a Dutch adoption magazine: "It is certainly an intense and important period in your life and well worth thinking long and hard about. You can emerge from it strengthened and enriched if you are willing and able".

So what have you discovered about yourself in the previous chapters? What moves you, what hurts you, what makes you sad? These are generally subjective experiences. A telephone conversation with a particular authority may have made you angry but the same conversation might not have affected someone else at all. A visit to a friend was disappointing for you, but it put someone else in a fantastic mood. It sounds strange and perhaps a little mean, but sadness, pain and disappointments are relative. Take a look at your relationship. You and your partner are probably upset, moved, angry and sad about the same things at different moments. One of you gets worked up while the other sits calmly reading a book. How is it that sadness is not the same for everybody, cannot be measured or predicted?

Because you are the one letting it in.

The moment you dare to recognise that you are in charge of your own thoughts, it means that they can also be influenced. It takes courage to acknowledge this fact. It used to be fashionable to talk of being "master of your own home". I would suggest it is far more worthwhile to strive to be "the master of your own mind". *You* determine whether and to what extent you want to feel sadness or if you will let it be. *You* determine whether and to what extent pain is allowed to dominate your life. I am certainly not promoting opening those drawers and stuffing something inside – that would render all the previous chapters meaningless. Nothing needs to end up in a drawer at all, it can stay in your mind, nicely tidied up. There will be plenty of space.

How and where should you start?

First of all, it is comforting to know that a wonderful technique has been devised to facilitate this process. It was originally called Rational Emotive Training, but has undergone a recent change of name and is now known as Rational Effectiveness Training. It was designed by Dr Albert Ellis, a psychotherapist who lived at the start of the previous century. He chose the direct approach instead of the psychoanalytical methods of the day which often dragged on for years. He showed that it is one's way of thinking which causes people problems or makes them ill. With the help of a strict scheme, he reflected people's behaviour and sought the pattern which ultimately came to light through the behaviour. Strikingly, the majority of underlying causes of undesirable behaviour appeared to originate in early childhood. Things we tend to joke about prove to be based on strict scientific evidence. I still think one should be able to make jokes about these aspects of oneself. I see myself as a cartoon figure with two blond plaits, perkily hopping on to a bus on the way to a nearby village to go to school, then spent hours crying there before making the homeward journey in the best of spirits. To be honest, it is quite funny, were it not for the fact that such an image from the past keeps creeping up on you in various disguises throughout the rest of your life. But if you recognise it you will be able to let it go and create room for other things.

Rational Effectiveness Training (RET)
How to work with RET.
RET is based on a simple ABC(D) scheme:
A = The event. This is what actually happens, for example, an unpleasant telephone conversation with an authority.
B = The thoughts that you have during the event: They cannot do that. I cannot handle this. This is scandalous.
C = The emotional reaction or the feelings: I felt angry, sad, afraid, I cried, I started a row with my husband.
D = Desirable behaviour in the face of the event.

It is a clearly set-out system that provides clarity. All you have to do is fill it in and then implement the clarity of the system step by step in your life. You normally begin with A, or occasionally with C if the emotion is so explosive that it seems more significant than the event causing it.

Let us take the example of the telephone conversation.
A = The adoption agency phones to say that the date of departure to collect your child from China has been postponed because of a SARS breakout and all journeys to the region are forbidden.
C = You start to cry, sink into a chair and are utterly upset for the rest of the day, you cannot sleep at night and you have to phone work to say you will not be coming in because you are unable to concentrate.

What causes the reaction C? Disappointment, for sure. Perhaps you had not been expecting such a thing at all, or perhaps you had an inkling because you had been watching the news. But has the world ended? No. Still, the disappointment is enormous. Is it the first time you react to a setback on your path in this manner? Answer this question by looking at several past events in your chest of drawers. If it is not the first time you react this way, this may well indicate a reaction pattern for you.

What could the Bs be, i.e. the thoughts?

B = erhaps we will never be able to go and collect her.

This is going to cause complications with the holidays I have booked off work.

My husband has to go to a conference later in the year.

Nothing ever works out for us.

It is terrible that this had to happen.

I will never get over this.

I always fail, I cannot even manage an adoption.

And so on, and so forth...

Then, take a look at every thought you have written down and for each thought, ask yourself a number of questions:

Is it realistic to think that the whole adoption will now fall through? Is it really true that the holiday request cannot be revised? Is it a drama to have to miss a conference and is it not a bit too soon to be bothering yourself with all these things at this stage anyway? Why is it such a terrible thing to happen? Why should you not get over it? Is it fair to say that you always fail? If you take an honest look at the questions you ask about your thoughts, you will conclude that it is not the event itself which has put you in such a state and left you lying lethargically on the settee, but rather your thoughts getting the better of you.

It is highly unrealistic to think that the adoption will never happen. And of course you do not always fail. In fact, do you ever fail – what does "fail" mean anyway? (new A) and why should you not get over it? Of course you will.

The next step is D. First check that you have described the details of the event (A) correctly. Look at it as if you were an outsider trying to get a precise picture of what has happened. Then make sure that you have written down the event fully and correctly and check whether you have asked enough critical questions about your thoughts.

D: What would be desirable behaviour? How would you like to feel after a telephone call like that? Of course there will be total disappointment as you had hoped to be leaving soon, and you had made all sorts of preparations for the big event. You will vent your frustration in your own way before realising that it is not, in fact, the end of the world, and then you can start taking stock of the situation and planning the next few practical steps.

I realise as I write this, that it all sounds very straightforward and matter-of-factly. To clarify: RET does not stand for: no emotions, nor for: no crying, nor for: no anger. RET aims to help you see that you yourself are in control of your own way of thinking.

Apply the RET approach to a number of individual events and you will see a pattern emerging in your way of dealing with things in life. As humans, we each tend to deal with things that happen to us in a way which is most comfortable for us. I cry, the little girl in the back of my mind, and you will have your own personal pattern. The big question is the icing on the cake: Why is it that you always have C reactions to your B questions? In the example, it is mainly fear which underlies the thoughts – but why is it that an event should make you afraid, or angry, sad, listless or hyperactive? Ellis comes to the conclusion that this is due to patterns adopted very early on in childhood.

Using the RET method to reveal your pattern is an important investment. It will help you realise that the long adoption procedure was a very valuable time.

Never throw away the ABCD systems, for they can help you look at the lessons you have taught yourself. After all, we are only human and tend to revert to old patterns. According to the scientific theory above, you will have to repeat the ABCD method two hundred times before you can cast off an old pattern and take on a new one. Let it be a challenge to achieve this a little sooner.

An exercise to realise the effect of an innocuous event on people's thoughts:

Imagine standing at a supermarket check-out. In front of you are two customers with full trolleys. Behind you an elderly couple are talking. What thoughts do you have at this moment as you stand waiting, and what thoughts might the others have? Imagine all sorts of other people with different backgrounds. It is clear that the young mother, the hectic businesswoman, the boys who are playing truant, the mayor's wife, the tourist, the man in a divorce, and the woman with the two whining toddlers will all have completely different thoughts and show different behaviour.

By becoming aware of this relativity you can "save" yourself, even in the adoption period.

Mourning

'Whenever I sit in a church, a child's baptism still brings tears to my eyes. We will never have the chance to experience this wonderful moment because our child was baptised in his native country.'

'Sometimes I feel like kicking myself when I cry over television programmes about giving birth. We have such a wonderful child now, even if she did not grow in my womb… All those feelings of powerlessness over my own body come rising to the surface again.'

When does the mourning stop, when have you cried enough? When do you cease to be caught off guard by a past feeling of sadness you thought you had come to terms with and had learnt to deal with? When will no more tears well up when you see a baby die in a film and suddenly find yourself reliving your own pain? When will you cease to feel a pang in your heart when you hear people talking about the pain a failed IVF attempt caused them? How is that at the most unexpected moments you can be overcome by a feeling of intense fatigue when you think back over four, five, ten years of medical manipulation without the beautiful result of a baby from your own pregnancy? When have you finally succeeded in saying goodbye to a dream? And above all: should you have to say goodbye at all? Is it necessary or desirable to put past moments of pain behind you once and for all? Should we allow sadness over what we have lost?

Loss is a part of life. There is no avoiding the experience. A toddler will lose or break toys. An older child may lose a friend who moves house. A teenager will discover the pain of that first separation after a broken-up relationship. A grandmother or grandfather will die, perhaps at a fairly young age, or even a parent, brother, sister or child. One can also lose a job, a dream, one's good health or the possibility to conceive a child.

The extent to which loss is connected to pain depends on how attached we were to what we lose. There can be a big difference between a two-year-old child losing its favourite soft toy on the beach or an adult losing a dull library book, to name an extreme example. The loss of a grandmother you saw once a year or a neighbour who looked after you every week will give rise to quite different feelings. Once someone said to me: 'I dare not think about my mother dying. I will not know what to do without her.' We had a long conversation about it at the time. On the one hand, it is a wonderful thing to be able to say how unbearably painful it would be to lose your mother; it shows how much she means to you and how much you love her. On the other hand, it is highly likely, and in fact desirable, that she should die before her children. I myself have learned a lot from my father's sudden death. It made me aware of the fact that parents *will* die and that I have to deal with the loss and carry on with my life. And however painful it is (how I would love to have him over for coffee and tell him: "Dad, I am fine, can you see how well I am doing? Look, I have now even got two children..."), you have to realise that there is no bringing anyone back from the dead. But it is precisely because I loved him that I am able to feel this way. So I now cherish what I still have more than I used to. I realise as I sit drinking coffee at my mother's that these so familiar, so intimate moments of the mother-daughter relationship will also come to an end. But then I realise that I will be allowed to continue to live and pass on what I have learned to our children.

But the grief for my father, is it over? Have I really put it behind me? Why do I get a lump in my throat as I write this?

Because I loved him. Other people who were important in my life have also died, but I no longer feel any pain from the loss. They were obviously not important enough in my life for me to mourn them for long. The loss of others, however, who seemed to be on the sidelines of my life, still bring me to tears. I still feel the pain, which in a way is wonderful.

Some friends have disappeared. Some partings were more painful than others. It was all a matter of intensity, sometimes the painful awareness that you do not want to or cannot be someone's friend or lover any longer. Sometimes you developed differently or just grew apart, which made things less painful.

Some other material things have also disappeared from my life. This generally does not upset me very much; I obviously do not get too attached to material things.

My chances of getting pregnant also disappeared. I am now at the start of the menopause and will never experience the miracle of a pregnancy. For years people kept telling me: "Just wait till the stress wears off a bit and you will get pregnant soon enough. I have read it so many times." That may well be…

I get tears in my eyes when someone near to me tells me about their trouble trying to get pregnant. And yet I now have my beautiful children. I cannot say I that would not have liked to carry my own children now that I have our children from Kenya in my heart and in my home. I do feel very strongly that these children were meant for us, that they crossed our path to join us on this journey through life. I believe in the guidance of God, the Almighty. But this does not change the fact that I often wonder when my infertility will stop having an emotional effect on me.

When does mourning end?
Personally, I have come to the conclusion that it never stops. It only changes; the degree of grief and sadness evolves. And what is most important for me: grief makes one grow. Not in the first hour or on the first day, and sometimes not even in the first few years. But if you can accept the grief and your loss, you can grow. To assist in this process:
Allow yourself to feel and experience pain, sadness and anger.
Do not idealise the old situation.
Do not freeze the old situation (extreme examples of this are never changing or tidying a deceased child's bedroom).
Look among friends and family for a shoulder to cry on.
Stay alert to physical symptoms, especially within the first two years after the loss. Perhaps you are stuck in the mourning process.

For many people, the start of the adoption period marks the end of their medical nightmare. Sometimes it marks the decision to no longer want or dare to get pregnant again after a difficult period of miscarriages and/or infant deaths. Be quite clear of the fact that once you and your partner have decided together to adopt, the child *will* come. But remember, too, that you must mourn the children you lost and those you never managed to conceive so that you can grow in the parenthood of the child which will be born in and of your heart.

Get yourself fit

Adopting is not something you can train for, however much you might like to. Even if you have already adopted one child and are now embroiled in the procedure to adopt the second or third, the terrain you have to cover will be riddled with surprises. It is a misconception to think that the second or third adoption will be easier than the first, for each adoption is unique.

To illustrate this, I would like to use the metaphor of muscular pains.

If you go out walking without training first, at some point you will get muscular pains, and if you see the adoption period as a long walk, it would be advisable to train in advance to prevent these pains. It does not take much to get muscular pains. What makes adoption so special in comparison with being pregnant is the length of the period and the uncertainty of the date on which the child is due. We are not talking about being two weeks overdue, when the doctor can intervene and induce the birth. We are talking about a period of several years which can easily be extended by a year beyond the original (expected) final date. As things stand in 2006, adoption procedures can easily take four to five years.

Fortunately, people who plan to adopt generally have the appropriate character for the task. Human beings can roughly be divided into two groups: people who do not like too much action and change and people who are active and like movement. A survey showed that the group of prospective adoptive parents consisted mainly of the latter. A welcome disposition, but also a dangerous one.

Throughout the long period spanned by adoption, things in your life can change on many different levels that call on you to be physically and mentally fit. In the field of typical adoption pitfalls alone, the scale is almost inexhaustible. Here are a number of examples:

Every country from which a child is to be adopted can change its adoption laws. The documents are subject to change. An infectious disease can break out. The child whose photo is already on display in your house could become seriously ill. The country can lower the maximum age for adoption. It can also close its borders – et cetera. In addition, changes in your immediate environment may lead to many unexpected twists and turns and place demands on your condition, such as the death of a loved one, moving house, falling ill, being made redundant, undergoing an operation or even becoming pregnant. We experienced many upheavals ourselves and I also read this in the reports that I received.

There was a tale of parents who had had the photo of their child on their mantelpiece for over a year before they could go and collect the child. The child gets older, the parents start to worry as the waiting seems to drag on indefinitely and yet you feel that you are *almost* there. Or the parents who were on the brink of setting off to collect their child when the dreaded SARS broke out. The new date was postponed for months. Just when you think you are nearly there, you suddenly find you have a whole way still to go. That gives you muscular pains.

You also get muscular pains from having to run around organising things. Phoning someone again, going to another office to get a certain document or have something stamped or signed. A fax has to be sent and an e-mail written. An accumulation of short movements can end up causing strain and muscular pains. It is not just the mental effort required to find new creative solutions again and again; it is also the physical effort that is required of you.

Your shoulders start to feel stiff, you feel empty inside and exhausted, but it is hard to be fully aware of this. The gradually accumulated tension keeps building up because you might automatically accommodate it and not feel it growing, or instead you might experience what you see as unrelated symptoms. And this is only because you did not recognise the initial signals. You do not feel the first signs of excessive tension because your sights are set unwaveringly on your goal of adopting a child. The danger is that everything else has to move out of the way as you focus only on this goal. Nothing is allowed to divert you from your path. And there lies the danger. You become absorbed in the major and minor events you see as leading you towards the adoption, whether this is the case or not. The accumulated muscular pains are the result of the small, individual events merging to become one huge indefinable mass. It develops when you see no end to the quantity and variety of feelings by which you are overcome during the adoption period. The result is that apparently unrelated symptoms emerge to alert you to the fact that you are neglecting to relax.

The following types of symptoms may emerge besides muscular pains:

Behavioural changes such as:
More of everything (food, drink, cigarettes, sweets, medicine, movement – for example at night in the form of grinding your teeth).
Less of everything (sleep, sense of humour, interest in the outside world, sex).

Emotional changes:
More of everything (anger, irritability, depression, tension, worry, crying, dreaming).
Less of everything (tolerance, interest in sex, memory and concentration).

Physical changes:
More of everything (headaches, muscular pains, allergies, skin irritations, PMT, stomach/digestive problems, susceptibility to illness, cardiac and vascular problems).
Less of everything (energy).

As with most symptoms, and also with muscular pains, the real pain is only really felt once you are at rest. You generally do not feel muscular pains during the physical activity but after several minutes or hours of rest. Our daughter unwittingly pointed this out after the second night of her skiing holiday: "Mummy, I slept so well that my legs hurt." When you get up again, you feel your muscles protesting. In adoption terms this occurs once the child is part of the family and you can relax and the tension is finally released. Physical symptoms in particular may slumber for years after the arrival of the child before manifesting themselves.

It is easier to understand when taking the process of lactic acid accumulation in the muscles and apply it to a wider context.

Due to the continuous state of concentration during the long adoption period, the body is in a permanent state of alertness at a micro level. You may not realise this as you have mentally prepared yourself for a long wait. You tell yourself and perhaps your partner in a moment of weakness that you must not complain – you knew what you were letting yourself in for…

The training consists mainly of learning to compensate tension with relaxation, for example with micro-breaks. These should be interspersed with larger breaks such as a weekend away, either alone or preferably together, so that you establish a sense of balance. Relax in a way that feels natural to you, either individually or as a couple. Or if you feel the need for action, do something mad and wild. Distract yourself from your normal everyday routine. Do not think that you are being childish. And above all, do not underestimate what long-term, undesirable stress can do to you.

Many studies have been carried out to examine the effects of positive and negative stress and active and passive stress. One of the studies consisted of two different tests performed on a group of 34 male students. The first test had them learn a certain subject matter by heart, after which they were given a twelve-minute test on what they had learned. The second test had them watch a twelve-minute film of footage of repulsive medical operations.

The difference was in the activity during the two tests. In the first test the students were actively involved and could influence the results. In the second test they had to watch passively. A saliva test was then performed and showed an increase in the concentration of defence proteins (which are a large part of the protective coating of organs). In the second test, the passive test, the concentration of these proteins decreased.

As well as looking for a way to avoid falling prey to passive or active stress, you can also become clearer about your goal. Even though you may not know anything about your future child, the following exercise may help:

> *Draw a picture of your future dream child. It does not have to be a work of art, it just needs to be drawn from your heart. Put the drawing in a frame and put it in a place which has a special meaning for you. This may be in the bedroom, outside in the corner of the garden, on the mantelpiece or wherever, as long as it is a special place. Decorate the space around the picture in a way that makes you feel good. Place a flower, a candle, a souvenir from your wedding anniversary trip or a photo of your family by the drawing. It does not actually matter what you choose, as long as you are happy with the final effect.*
>
> *This way, you create an image of your 'medal', your final goal. You can use this place to enjoy the silence and listen to yourself, or to withdraw to together with your partner, to meditate or just to look at the drawing and remind yourself when things are not running smoothly: this is why we are doing all this!*

In our case, we had seen our children independently of each other from their fifth and fourth month respectively. We had photos in the room, we had hours of footage, the children had already been integrated into our lives by family and friends. In fact, it was almost too real, but we would not have it any other way. The risk was very real (and things did indeed almost go wrong) that our child in the photograph would remain but a dream. But it kept us on our toes.

The drawing comes straight from your heart, a beautiful reflection of your dream which will one day become a reality.

Company

'In the middle of our adoption procedure we met other couples who were also in the throes of adoption. Now that we have our children with us we realise that this time brought us much closer to them, as we laughed together, made bad jokes together, cried together.'

'It's great to be understood without having to explain yourself.'

Adopting is not a great social event. Despite being together, you often feel alone. Whereas pregnant women get together for yoga and swimming for expectant mothers, there are no such activities on offer for expectant adoptive parents. It is also difficult to explain what problems you are having because so few people have any first-hand experience with the hazards of adoption. No one can see how long you have been waiting, you do not get any fatter or less mobile and no one gives up their seat for you on the bus. You are absorbed by something that has major implications on your life, but no outsider can see what is going on.

The big question is: does this really matter?

The results of the survey showed that family and friends were a great source of support, but often only to a certain degree. Fortunately, there generally is plenty of sympathy from these fronts: these are people who may have seen you worry or know only too well how you wish to mean something to a child from another country. Another point that was often quoted in the survey on the subject of support was the comfort derived from the joint journeys to China to collect the adoptive children. They were like a party, everyone equally excited, everyone equally uncertain, everyone happy at the same moment, followed by the journey home together. When you feel this exhilaration, this blissful feeling of finally being united with your child, you understand why you went through it all.

It appears to be highly desirable to share experiences. It makes us feel good and almost all groups of adoptive parents organise reunions for many years afterwards, reuniting the children and taking group photos.

In view of the desirability to meet people in a similar situation, adoptive parents get a raw deal. Only if you are lucky you meet people who are also going through the processes at that exact moment. Although a few hundred adoptions are finalised in the Netherlands every year, this is a very small percentage when spread over the entire Dutch population. Another factor is that each adoption differs greatly from the next, so even if you do know other people who are trying to adopt, it will be surprising if they are going through quite the same feelings, tension and frustration as you are.

Independent adopters are often complete soloists when it comes to the adoption period. Don Quichote versus the bureaucratic stronghold. They have different problems, as they suffer from rumours about bypassing the law and getting involved in semi-legal activities abroad. Yet in reality, such people are generally especially concerned about the poorest children. They often have some kind of experience with the country of their choice, perhaps through friends who work in a third-world country, as a result of which they have come into contact with orphaned children there. They are often highly motivated, enthusiastic people, who have a clear idea of what they want. Due to their lack of knowledge of the legal system in the adoptive country of their choice, they often find themselves fighting a lonely battle in the Netherlands and also abroad in the quest to adopt a child from the country they have so consciously selected.

While we were struggling to bring Mette's adoption to a successful conclusion, it was wonderful for us to meet a couple who were also trying to adopt a child from that orphanage. At the time, they actually lived but a few kilometres from our village. This brought some relief to the difficult days we were having, trying to get things organised. It also gave us the energy to help others and share our experiences.

Why share your experiences?

First of all, there is *recognition*. Fill a room with bald men, and one immediately sees what they have in common. A man with a full head of hair would stand out. The sense of all sharing a particular characteristic creates serenity through equality. Gather a group of pregnant women together, and it is obvious what the topic of conversation is going to be. It would be surprising to hear them all talking about their choice of reading glasses. Put these women's partners in the room next door and it is possible that a stranger might not recognise what they have in common, as there is no externally visible indicator to aid the recognition.

When people are familiar with your feelings, you feel confident enough to tell them about these feelings. How often do you experience someone really understanding how long things are taking and that you sometimes lie awake for hours from the uncertainty?

There is a good chance that within a group of people sharing your problems, you will see nods and hear sighs of recognition as you tell them about your feelings. You are not alone, you and your feelings are fully understood.

You can *exchange experiences*. It can be such a wonderful feeling to air your experiences without having to give any additional explanations. You can also learn from others in the same situation. How do they deal with the problems that also face you? Or how did they handle the problems that you are now encountering?

You can *learn from each other*. It is an indisputable fact that you are more willing to accept advice from someone who has been in the same position than from an outsider. If you feel like you have hit rock bottom at some point and there seems to be no light at the end of the tunnel, a well-meaning family member can easily say that you should not worry so much but chances are his well-intended advice will not be heeded. What does he know? If you vent your frustration about the situation to someone well versed in adoption, a fellow-sufferer, the feeling of hopelessness you seem to be stuck in will take on a new dimension, as will the advice that this person might give you. From someone experienced in the matter you will generally more willingly take advice than from someone disconnected from the issue. This is what makes coming together with other adoptive parents so special. There is a lot to learn from each other and opinions and advice more easily accepted.

You can *support and guide each other*. It often does you the world of good to be on the receiving end of a warm gesture, a kind letter or a heartfelt remark. Warmth, affection, humour, an open ear, a gentle suggestion can make all the difference. Support does not always have to consist of agreeing with another's point of view. It can also take the form of gently correcting a misguided action or thought within an environment of trust. This enables you to see new openings and sheds a new light on how you can deal with the problems you are facing. Within an environment of trust, among people sharing the same experiences, it is often possible to achieve more productive results than you could achieve with outsiders, however close to you they may be.

You can *laugh with each other*. During the VIA course, we often availed ourselves of a dark sense of humour on the subject of our infertility or our choice of adoptive country. We spoke our own language, had our own humour. An outsider would not have understood and may well have mistaken us for heartless barbarians. Yet it was safe to use this humour within the group. We knew everyone's underlying pain and therefore ridiculed each other and ourselves. My husband and I thought this was wonderful. It often replenished our energies.

Choosing and being chosen

- You choose a job…
- You choose a partner…
- You choose a house…
- You choose a car…
- You choose a holiday…
- You choose to love yourself…
- You choose to lead a healthy life…
- You choose to have a child…?

To an extent, you can buy whatever you want and make happen whatever you want. Matters of health can of course only partially be influenced by a person. The choice to have children is far trickier.

Everyone learns to make choices from an early age. Children choose presents for their birthdays or Christmas. They choose a sport or a hobby, later on they choose a school, college or university, and so on. An important aspect when making a good choice is how weighing up the various possibilities makes you feel. Ideally, you will ask yourself: what do I WANT to choose and what CAN I choose? In other cases, for example when a diabetic is choosing a meal on a menu, an important question will be: what MAY I choose? In certain situations the question: what MUST I choose? could come up.

Obligations cause stress. An obligation implies the absence of choice. Not having the freedom to choose can cause great unhappiness. A look at the Holmes stress list makes it clear that most things that cause stress are related to some kind of compulsion, which could be imposed by nature (death, illness), work (redundancy), by matters that will not go away (financial upheaval such as heavy debts) or inter-relational situations (divorce).

Louise Hay asks her clients to write a list of the things they *have to* do in their life. What do you consider your own obligations to be and above all, why do you feel these obligations?

Revealing word games can be played with the words want, can, must and may. These word games say a lot about how one has been brought up, how one looks at things in life and what baggage one has accumulated throughout life. Using the question 'why' you can approach a theme in a number of different ways:

- Why may you not do what you can do?
- Why do you want to do something you cannot do?
- Why must you do what you do not want to do?
- Why may you not do what you want to do?
- Why do you not do what you want to do?

The list can be extended, but the idea is clear.

If you would like a child but find yourself involuntarily childless, the moment comes that you say to yourself: I WANT to bear a child, but I CANNOT. The choice you would have wanted no longer applies. For people who decide to fulfil their wish for a child in a different way, the word WANT takes on a significant role. And using the above words you get the following construction:

We WANT a child, we CANNOT have one the normal way, (question addressed to the Ministry of Justice:) MAY we adopt a child with your permission?, (answer from the ministry:) yes, but you MUST wait a long time.

The word 'must' has negative connotations for most people. This is understandable, because the word 'must' is the word of authority, it is something which is imposed upon you, exerts force on you, and makes you powerless.

The big question is now: how can I change the sentence and remove the word 'must', the element of obligation? Obligation makes us sad, angry and desperate. I 'had to' finish my plate when I was young (I was sent to the shed if I left anything), I 'had to' go to school by bike although it was raining, some people 'had to' go to church, study a certain subject, get married – had to, had to, had to…

'Having to' causes feelings of pain and stress.

It hurts a lot less if the 'having to' can be transformed into 'wanting to'. However difficult – and believe me, I know – you would be able to read the sentence differently and then it would eventually hurt less. It has to do with accepting the inevitable. It is related to the RET therapy mentioned in a previous chapter.

If you want to adopt a child in the Netherlands – and the same applies to many other countries – you know that you are going to need a great deal of patience. Unlike the slow medical process of going from one procedure to the next and from one type of hormone to another year after year, adoption is different. One does not register for adoption to think, years later: "Wow, four years and still no baby". That kind of waiting and wanting and not being able to are behind you. The problem of waiting for years also applies to people who decide to adopt on idealistic grounds, so I do realise that now, my reasoning is slightly flawed. And yet you cannot blot out all those years of repeated attempts and sweating it out between laboratory results. They make you all the more sensitive and impatient. But the word 'must' does not bring you any closer. The word 'want' does.

The word 'want' is powerful. Dutch motivator and positivist Emile Ratelband applies it to his life. Some see him as a guru and others see him as a charlatan. He *does* what he wants. The same applies to adoptive parents: they do what they want. They want a child and they go for it. Always bear in mind that the will is strong and that it *will* happen. When you become aware of the positive energy emitted by the word 'want' then you will come to cherish this word. Energy, life energy, adds color and sheen to your life and makes you strong.

It can help you to visualise what you want. In practical terms, you could put up a photo in your house of something that makes you think of the country from which you want to adopt. The photo could depict a Brazilian image of Christ, colourful girls from India, a touching street scene from China or a white smile in a black face from Africa. You could reserve a corner in your home to collect souvenirs from that country. In a less tangible way you could visualise what you want through meditation or prayer.

Wanting is positive. It is especially important to remain positive throughout the adoption period. The longer the fighting and waiting drags on, the more important it is to be able to remain positive. Avoid things which cost energy and cause stress. The people you choose to be with and the situations you put yourself in voluntarily should give you energy, not drain you of it. Do not forget that you are vulnerable in terms of the energy you have available, and make sure you share your feelings not only with your partner but also with family and friends.

It may also help to meet people in the same situation as yourself. Simply wanting the same thing can make you a great source of comfort to each other.

It is also important that you do not do anything you do not want to do. Keep asking yourself what your motivation is for doing something you do not want to do. Do not forget that this is sapping your energy and that energy is what you need most of all. And if you think it is selfish to do what you want, remember that your child is soon going to need you and that it will use your energy to bond, and feel loved and happy.

Choosing or being chosen

You are the ones doing the choosing. You choose to adopt, whatever your motivation. But there is also the aspect of being chosen. This is the child's choice.

People who know a bit about spirituality and cosmic energy generally view the subject of choosing and choices in a different way. It is not only you who are choosing a child; the child also chooses you. Many adoptive parents have difficulties with the fact that the adoption agency decides which child will ultimately take its place in your family and your heart. The matching procedure is an essential part of the agency's task. But this need not worry you quite so much. The energy in the universe is so strong that there are already waves of energy vibrating between child and parents which cannot be measured but do exist. The child who will ultimately become part of your family already chose you long ago. This may sound rather far-fetched, but when talking to other adoptive parents, they tend to confirm this most emphatically. In our case too, the match seems perfect.

What we learn from Mette, among many other things, is first and foremost to give love and be generous. From Wisse we learn to be patient and to give someone space to be himself. From other parents I hear similar stories. "When we went to China with the group and our girl was placed in my arms, I knew immediately that she belonged in our life. "Or: I had hoped that she would be for us, she was the most beautiful to me". The father of an older child said: "She climbed up on my wife's lap, threw her arms around her neck and rested her head on my wife's chest in total devotion".

Regardless of the circumstances, you can rest assured the child placed in your family has a message for you. It is meant to be with you and to grow with you into adulthood. Deepak Chopra writes in one of his books: "The claim that life is unfair implies that life is arbitrary, meaningless, erratic and dangerous, in other words: that there are no spiritual laws at work".

'We were in the unusual and unique position of being able to 'choose' our child. Or, as the orphanage put it: 'fall in love with her'. I picture the events in my mind as if they were a film, although we very consciously did not film it or take any photos. It felt very familiar and our daughter actually gave us the feeling that she had chosen us and

was our child from the very first moment. We never doubted having made the right choice, it was perfect. I would have moved heaven and earth to keep her'.

The first moment of contact is not always one of intense emotion. But I personally do not know of any adoptive parents who are not convinced that they have received the perfect child for them. Fortunately, almost all first moments of contact are indeed spontaneous, moving and unforgettable. Sometimes other problems come later on in the life of an adoptive child, but this has to do with things other than whether or not the child ended up in the right place. Many books have been written about problems with adoptive children in the long term, and in recent years far more expert guidance has become available for the adoptive child and its family due to the growing awareness of the importance of bonding and the causes and implications of the failure to bond. But this is not the intention of this book. I am, however, convinced that the more pleasant and positive the parents experience the adoption period to be, the more favourable the conditions will be for bonding and for the further development of the child. After all, children have a great capacity for picking up on subtle negative energy.

That far away country

At some point during the VIA information course the moment comes when the photos get passed around. But these are not family photos or photos of houses, gardens and streets of the couples in the group

These are photos of children from all parts of the world. Yellow, black, light and dark brown, white, red: a delightful array passes through your hands.

This is the moment of reality for many couples: *our* child will be coming from one of those countries. In a few years we will be setting off to one of those countries.

For us, choosing was a piece of cake. We knew exactly what we wanted, we knew the country and by the end of the course, we even knew our child-to-be. We loved Kenya and the Kenyans before we had the slightest inkling that we would one day adopt. Our house is full of giraffes, ebony figures, soapstone mother-and-child sculptures, and so on. On the wall in our living room is a gorgeous, warm painting from a lovely woman painter from Kenya.

For most couples, however, the choice was not so obvious. Yet the inevitable moment comes when you have to choose the country from which you would like to adopt a child. This may have far-reaching implications, but the choice can sometimes be quite a practical one. For example, a child from China will most likely be a girl. Columbia requires prospective adopters to free a certain period of time to spend in the country.

Why choose a particular country?

Perhaps its procedures are not too difficult. Perhaps you have worked there. Perhaps you find its children particularly beautiful. Perhaps you do not want to wait any longer. Perhaps your age might become an issue if you wait any longer. Perhaps adopting from that particular country is less expensive.

A choice of country is a choice for life. It may be helpful to familiarise yourself with the different options in advance. Visiting the country on holidays and speaking to the local people, perhaps even work together with them, can be invaluable when making your choice. In the Netherlands, it is possible to establish contact with people from India, China and Ethiopia to ask them about their cultures and countries.

It may also be helpful to read about the country. Many wonderful books have been written about all countries of the world and in particular about the people who live there, their characters and customs. It is a good idea to prepare yourself for these issues.

It is certain that your future child will come from a completely different world and culture than your own. A holiday in Spain does not take you outside of Europe, but nevertheless brings you to a land of a different speed and customs, where people have a completely different temperament from us Dutch. Imagine how much greater the differences will be in the countries from which most adoptions take place.

Collect some of the country's delicious recipes, let yourself be enchanted by its music (take a djembe course, for example), go to South African dance lessons, or find inner peace with Eastern meditation. You have all the time in the world, after all, plus it will help take your mind off the less enjoyable aspects of the adoption procedure and familiarise you with your future child's native culture.

What is even more important is the fact that you will soon be confronted with that other culture from the second you hold your child in your arms or it comes running up to you. A baby still feeding on only milk may not be very aware of the transition from one culture to another, but for infants and older children, the change should not be underestimated. You will have a major head start as a parent if during the long wait you immerse yourself in getting to know your future child's culture. There may still be plenty of other problems.

Before you set off to collect your child up, it is advisable to make a list of questions to ask when you arrive. Do not think that you will not need such a list – believe me, seeing your child for the first time, makes a person lose their ability to think clearly. You will be overcome by feelings you never had before.

A list will help you receive valuable information about your child's feeding habits (do not let them be presented to you as easier than they really are) and about things which your child is used to (bathing or no, cuddling or no, nappy or no, foods to avoid, toys or no) and ask about words in the local language ("good girl", "don't cry", or "I love you").

When you arrive home with your child, a whole new phase of the adoption period begins. It has not been completely finalised, but the worst is behind you: you now have a child! Try and give the child the space it needs to get used to its new surroundings. Crying, screaming, any form of expressing emotions: all is allowed, as discussed at the VIA course.

I would like to stress that the better prepared you are for such things, the more adept you will be at dealing with them. The same applies to the differences in culture. Eating with a spoon or a fork is probably a new phenomenon for many older children, and lemonade or sugar may well be a much-desired treat. Ice-cream is a feast. It is important to be aware that not only cultural differences but also differences such as undernourishment or malnourishment may pose serious problems if not appropriately addressed.

There are specialised doctors who can advise you on these matters.

For every child from another culture there is also the issue of physical contact. When adopting a child, you might encounter problems associated with emotional neglect. In Geertje van Egmond's book *Bodemloos Bestaan* ('Bottomless Existence'), she describes this syndrome as an emotional handicap which arises from physical and emotional neglect in early childhood. An unhappy prenatal period is also quoted as a cause of emotional damage in the long run. We know, for example, that Wisse would lie in his own urine during the first months of his life and certainly did not receive much personal attention or love. We know that Mette spent the first months of her life among other children in incubators. Mette is a child who flourishes most in the company of others. Does this come from the incubator period? Or is this just part of her nature? Wisse cannot feel if he has wet his trousers and can easily run around all day in wet underpants if he is too absorbed in playing and forgets to go to the toilet.

We might easily have found ourselves in a situation where Wisse had actually been spoilt rotten at the orphanage or had been given his way in everything. Something which may not be expected. But once we had Wisse with us for good, we clearly noticed that he always expected our undivided attention. Fortunately, we had already seen signs of this at the orphanage: at the slightest whinge someone lifted him on to their lap. I personally believe that you cannot give a baby too much affection, but Wisse, already fifteen and a half months, was a toddler and had to start learning that he could not do everything he wanted. We were luckily alerted to this aspect of Wisse's character by a social worker and with a gentle touch and plenty of love, we were able to establish a sense of equality between him and his sister.

Unfortunately, the opposite is true in a large majority of cases. This morning, for instance, I heard the sad story of a Korean child lying in a cot with a hole in the side through which a teat had been stuck for the child to suckle on. It reminded me of the hamsters in the cage at the local pet shop and I immediately thought that the hamsters fared better, for they have children coming by to pick them up and stroke them.

Soon your child will arrive in your family, with little or a lot of baggage in its backpack, with great or small problems adapting, a major or a minor culture difference. As a couple, you have all the time in the world during the adoption period. So go out and find out about that other culture, the homeland of your future child.

Profile sketch of an adoptive parent

It is amusing to note that adoptive parents generally have a number of characteristics in common. Just as you see similarities in certain jobs, you also see them in adoptive parents. There are those certain types who become nurses, teachers, doctors, pilots, accountants, waiters, artists, managers, et cetera. You can spot them a mile off.

The characteristics of adoptive parents make them strong and vulnerable at the same time. Adoptive parents-to-be have been shown to be phenomenally forthright when it comes to achieving their goals. In their case, such assertiveness is a virtue without which they would never manage to reach the goal they have set for themselves. They generally also have a strong personality and are highly active. This is one reason why the waiting is so terrible for them. They like to stay in control of things, both big and small. They are result-orientated, take up a struggle if necessary, have a keen sense of justice and want to achieve the best results.

Their homes are often very tidy (not necessarily excessively clean) so that they have a clear picture of where things are. They expect a lot from themselves, but also of others. They do not take things lightly, are critical, deep thinkers and will always think things over carefully before making a decision. These are people of principles with which they will not readily part. They may well have a rather dark sense of humour, possibly the result of their experiences with adoption.

Despite the knowledge that I will likely be criticised for it, I have drawn up a character sketch of the typical adoptive parent. I do wonder how it is that the majority of adoptive parents to whom I show this sketch, recognise themselves to some extent.

Could the answer lie in the fact that so many of them have been through all those years of fighting for a child?

Could it be that this group of people will not accept any misfortune without putting up a fight because that is precisely what they have been doing for years, so they just keep going on the chosen path in the quest for a child? Is it fate that these people go through life childless?

These questions I cannot answer. I recently spoke about involuntary childlessness with a close friend. She said: 'I know that you two would have accepted it in the end. You would have found a new way together.' I am not so sure myself. What I do know is that there is a choice. Either you embark on a new way, or you perish from the misery of missing what you cannot have.

Either you seek a new source of love for something, something you can share, or you find all the sources have dried up and offer only bitterness and harshness.

That was not a choice we had to make, although during the medical procedures in the hospital, we did become increasingly involved in our joint passion: natural healthcare.

Do you recognise yourself or your partner in this character sketch?

If so, you can elaborate on each characteristic mentioned above and imagine where it could lead in a period as difficult as the one on the way to adoption. Once you have arrived at this chapter it the time is right for the following exercise:

Make a list of characteristics you see in yourself and leave at least two lines empty after each characteristic. Do not be too hard on yourself and make sure you include positive characteristics. It appears that our type (adoptive parents) find it far easier to write down negative characteristics than positive ones. You then write in the first empty line why this characteristic could pose a danger to you during the adoption period. In the second empty line you write an alternative.

Example:
Characteristic: Very assertive.
Danger: Do not know where to stop, cannot restrain myself.
Alternative: I could work on letting go.

Another example:

Characteristic:	Sense of justice.
Danger:	Cannot handle injustice.
Alternative:	I must realise that I might have the feeling (whether justified or not) that injustice is done to me during the adoption procedure. This is almost inevitable. It will do me no good influencing me. I must accept the injustice (real or imagined).

As I sit thinking about characteristics typical of adoptive parents, the telephone rings. Believe it or not, it is another adoptive parent, a father.

I tell him what I am doing at the moment and half jokingly tell him about my character profile, aware that it sounds rather clichéd. At first he says nothing, then he says I have hit the nail on the head.

Once you have got to know yourself and your partner better by doing this exercise, you will be able to support each other more effectively when necessary. Each characteristic you write down is a part of you, but not every characteristic is conducive to assisting you in the adoption procedure. So look critically, and above all with humour, and it will help you grow.

A child of your own

During the adoption period, I had not given much thought to the fact that although the child would be my own, it would not have anything of mine in its genetic make-up. Although this book focuses primarily on the adoption period, this issue is still worth mentioning briefly, for it will play a role from day one of the meeting.

Parents who have had biological children were at birth confronted with the question of whom the child resembles. Deep in his heart, granddad hopes it looks like him or at least like grandma, and the same applies to the other set of grandparents. Similar comparisons are made as the child develops. Oh yes, you also walked quickly like that, look at that little hand, that is how you used to wave as a baby. Out of nappies in no time, his dad was just the same, walking slowly, he has got that from his dad, too. Breaking stuff, having tantrums, playing alone, always clinging to mother's skirt… do not worry now, dear, you did that for years, and see, you turned out fine.

As history teaches us that things have a way of working out, a young parent generally does not worry too much. The fact that a dear son goes around breaking things does not mean that he will not grow up to be a surgeon. The fact that a sweet daughter has been clinging to her mother's skirt for a year does not mean that she will not turn into a self-sufficient businesswoman. The fact that your child is unable to sit still for a moment does not mean you should rush off to consult a child psychologist. You used to be exactly the same, yet nowadays nothing makes you happier than reclining peacefully on the couch with a book.

The situation is somewhat different for adoptive parents.

They have no mirror, no reassuring word from a parent, no inner voice that says it will all be fine in the end.

No, you are dealing with a unique child with an identity entirely its own, of which you are totally unaware. This makes the job of directing, coaching and assisting without fear all the more challenging. I must say, I find it a difficult task and a heavy responsibility.

It is true that as time passes, I am becoming more confident and calmer in my approach to this task. But I still find it the hardest part of the whole adoption. How tolerant should you be towards a child that is naughty, rude, mean, tells white lies, claims its freedom, hides things from you, or wants your undivided attention?

When is behaviour normal for a child of that age, and when should you intervene?

Should you intervene at all or will you hinder the child in its identity? When I see two friends of mine with their shy child, I think that it is no wonder their son is also quiet and shy. But no one worries, because the parents are fantastic people and cope wonderfully with the jungle that is life.

It is best to be fully aware at the outset that your child comes into your life with its own inborn, ready-made uniqueness. It is tempting to want to give the child something of yourself. But what was good for you will not necessarily be good for the child in the same way. I actually think that the ultimate challenge of adoption is to bring out the best out in your child, its own nature and character always the priority. It is the quest for uniqueness, the most intimate part of the child. The aim is not to produce a copy of yourself or your partner, but to help a person flourish in his or her own right, a person who has a right to exist, only with genetic material no one knows anything about. Your upbringing and guidance can help you offer your values to your child within its own capacity.

That is the art of adoption.

Make yourself at home

There is something moving about arrival cards. They are a reflection of the desire, the struggle, and the intense joy at the ultimate arrival of the child. The adoptive child will later see the card and realise the significance of the message: You are ever so welcome, we wished for you so strongly!

Studies show that adoptive children, in the same way as other children, will at some point be confronted with their identity. This may happen in puberty, or earlier, sometimes not until they become pregnant themselves, but the moment will most probably come that they feel uncertain, sad, angry and unwanted.

You may well be thinking that you will cross that bridge when you come to it and for now prefer to concentrate on bringing the adoption procedure to a successful conclusion.

But it is not as simple as that. My mother used the Dutch saying: 'Good governance requires foresight' and in this way I became the organiser of many events inside and outside of the family.

During the procedure there are several things you can do to help make things easier for your child or children in the future. Because however loving, caring and so on you are as an adoptive parent, someone else, a woman, bore that child and did not want to, or could not, look after it and bring it up. A man other than the adoptive father supplied the sperm, yet is now no longer a part of the life of the adopted child. There is nothing you can do about that, but later it will be a source of sadness to your child.

What you can do is show your child how deeply you love him or her and also show willingness to search for his or her roots.

You can do this, for example, by keeping a diary of your own story of this special time and your desire to have this child from this country. As I already mentioned, there are many ways of familiarising yourself with your child's country of origin, of which I will name just a few: holidays, books about the country, travel books, stories of other people's travels, CDs or films from that country.

Open an account for monthly savings towards a journey with the whole family to take the child back to see where it was born.

We very carefully chose the names with which to baptise our children. Each child has three names so that they know they are equal. Both have their biological mother's (or as we say at home: belly mother) name. And both have names of great-grandparents from either side of the family, so that they feel a welcome part of both families. Mette's name means pearl and Wisse's means good. The choice of a name can also contribute to the child's feeling of being made welcome.

Do not forget to let those around you grow with the child from the different culture. Let parents, brothers, sisters and friends join in and if they are interested, tell them about the culture and customs of the child's country of origin. Do not forget that you and your partner grow towards the child far more quickly than those around you do. Talking about the child's culture and letting people get to know your child will help further the child's integration with its environment.

My mother once came to Nairobi with us before the adoption became part of our lives. She wanted to see the orphanages for which we did voluntary work and thus she also visited Nyumbani. She has extremely moving memories. She regularly talks to her grandchildren about her visit there and shows them photos of her on her visit to the orphanage. For the children, it is the most normal thing in the world. Grandma is part of their lives and they have no grasp of how special it was that plain old grandma should also be in photos of Nyumbani. It was wonderful to be able to do that. The same applies to friends from church, and colleagues from KLM, who can say: we have been there, at your orphanage, look at this photo. And our children cannot think of anything more exciting (except perhaps *Finding Nemo*) than the film that shows them as babies, growing up – so far away, yet in a way so close to home.

We hope that through our talks with our children they will not feel lost in their own world. But if it does help them, it will be thanks to the energy we put into it, not only during our preparation for the adoption but also, unknowingly, before we even knew we would try to adopt. I realise, of course, that we had a significant financial advantage due to our work, which brought Kenya much closer. But I am convinced that in the same way that many roads lead to Rome, so do many different ways lead to all the different countries in the world from which children are adopted.

I hope that you can find a way that is right for you.

Final growth

During this year's summer holidays, we pitched our tent at a campsite in the Netherlands. Although we were both working throughout the school holidays (the risk of working in shifts), we were able to work alternately and thus still find time to spend some time camping together as a family. After a few days, someone at the campsite approached us. 'They' had been talking about us. 'They' had enjoyed watching how we all got on together, how we interacted with the children but also with each other as a couple. 'They' could see that we were a special team.

Goodness.

Sometimes my husband and I are hardly aware of the intense bond that has resulted from the events of the past years. The adoption period certainly helped us grow together as a couple, but so did the other events that happened during that time and profoundly affected our personal lives. They made us more tolerant towards each other, and now one word sometimes suffices for either of us to know what the other means. Despite being two totally different people, we feel equal. We have every bit of respect for those differences, because by complementing each other we help each other to grow.

Ask adoptive parents if the adoption period itself benefited them in any way, and the question is usually met with hesitation, followed by a whole list of positive points. I have spoken to parents who ended up saying they would not have missed it for the world and would advise every parent to adopt a child, if only to emerge from the experience as a stronger person (adoption agencies would not be pleased with this suggestion).

Here is a selection of reactions from people who participated in the survey:

> "The fact that we managed this whole thing together. It was so good to have a joint goal to gradually work towards."

> "I have discovered that you mustn't sweep any hidden messages under the carpet, they'll be back to cause trouble later. One look at my wife and I know exactly what's up. I now also find it easier to deal with the emotional side of my nature. As a man, it's almost impossible to get through the adoption period with dry eyes."

> "On the one hand, I have learned to dedicate myself to something I really want, and make sure I get it. On the other hand, I still find it difficult to resign myself to some inevitable things that I come across in life."

> "When I was in the middle of the period of all the hospital visits, I often felt angry and helpless because things weren't going as I'd hoped. Looking back on all those years, I think it was always meant to be that we would adopt our children. I have become calmer in life and more trusting of the fact that things are supposed to happen as they do."

> "We are now far more aware of what we do with our lives and see the riches of life itself. Many of the questions we longed to find an answer to in the past, we now view from quite a different perspective."

> "What I found particularly positive was the wish, the longing, the sharing and the whole process of growing together towards a child that isn't your own flesh and blood. We could help each other when one of us was fed up with all the regulations and bureaucracy."

How can it be that so much misery and stress can bring you emotional growth? I would say: you have no choice. You are so emphatically confronted with the fact that what you have in your hands is all relative, that you are bound to come out of it better or worse.

It is impossible to emerge from the experience unchanged.

My survey did not give an indication of how many people had given up at some point during the procedure. Some people who participated in the survey were still in the process of trying to adopt, but the majority had since adopted one or more children from a special place in the world.

We human beings like to try and keep things under control. But when the desire to have children falls outside of the category of things you can control, slowly but surely you will find yourself entering quite a different world. It is as though the moment of truth has arrived. You are confronted with your inability to shape events as you would like. This can be an enormous blow, but it can also be the first step towards change.

Life is movement. When you stop moving, you are dead. It is impossible that you should be born, go to school, go to work, retire and say on your deathbed that nothing's changed since your birth. You would surely have missed the point. As life is continuing movement, one has to move with it, or find the current against them.

The trick is to find the right current for you. Marianne Williamson writes that surrender does not diminish our power, but merely strengthens it.

Only when you become aware of of the fact that you have to let things go in order to move on, you will be able to move on. Sometimes you come up against exactly the same type of problem (you repeatedly lose control over things, like infertility, redundancy from work, health) and you ask yourself why it has to happen to you. What have I done to deserve this? It is not fair. Chérie Carter-Scott wrote a remarkable book about her vision on life.

The essence of her message is: life teaches you just enough lessons you need to live your life. Only when you understand that something in your life happens from which you have something to learn and only if you take the lesson to heart will you actually change your approach to life. Buddha said: 'Learn to let go. That is the key to happiness.'

The very fact of being alive implies changes of all kinds, but a whole new influx of changes will come into play during the years of the adoption period. Particularly in the beginning, you will find the current speeding up and you might not recognise the full implications of the sensation. But the current will carry you to your child, a wonderful child, a child who is perhaps waiting for you somewhere in the world at this very moment. Many new people will cross your path. People you have been waiting for, people you expect and people you had rather run away from. There will be people who will accompany you part of the way, friends, relatives, colleagues. But there will also be people who walk a path parallel to yours and of whom you slowly but surely lose sight. This happens in life in general, but it could also happen to you in your life as adoptive parents. You are both entering a phase of growth, sometimes at such a high speed that a third party would not be able to keep up. But you need this growth to be there for your child.

You need to make a strong team, a foundation on which a child can build a home.